HOW TO BUY FOOD
For Economy and Quality

HOW TO BUY FOOD
For Economy and Quality

Recommendations of the
UNITED STATES DEPARTMENT OF AGRICULTURE

DOVER PUBLICATIONS, INC., NEW YORK

Published in Canada by General Publishing Company, Ltd., 30 Lesmill Road, Don Mills, Toronto, Ontario.
Published in the United Kingdom by Constable and Company, Ltd., 10 Orange Street, London WC 2.

How to Buy Food for Economy and Quality, first published by Dover Publications, Inc. in 1975 contains corrected reprints of the following United States Department of Agriculture Home and Garden Bulletins: No. 201, *How to Buy Dairy Products*, August, 1972; No. 193, *How to Buy Cheese*, September, 1971; No. 144, *How to Buy Eggs*, January, 1968; No. 177, *How to Buy Dry Beans, Peas, and Lentils*, June, 1970; No. 143, *How to Buy Fresh Vegetables*, December, 1967; No. 198, *How to Buy Potatoes*, February, 1972; No. 167, *How to Buy Canned and Frozen Vegetables*, April, 1969; No. 141, *How to Buy Fresh Fruits*, October, 1967; No. 191, *How to Buy Canned and Frozen Fruits*, August, 1971; No. 146, *How to Buy Beef Roasts*, January, 1968; No. 145, *How to Buy Beef Steaks*, February, 1968; No. 157, *How to Buy Poultry*, July, 1968; No. 195, *How to Buy Lamb*, August, 1971; No. 166, *How to Buy Meat for Your Freezer*, December, 1969.

International Standard Book Number: 0-486-21913-5
Library of Congress Catalog Card Number: 74-26000

Manufactured in the United States of America
Dover Publications, Inc.
180 Varick Street
New York, N.Y. 10014

CONTENTS

HOW TO BUY FOOD
For Economy and Quality

How to Buy DAIRY PRODUCTS

Milk is an excellent source of calcium, protein, and riboflavin, and contains many other vitamins and minerals as well. It also supplies fat and sugar. Getting enough milk should be a pleasure. This booklet can help you shop wisely for the whole array of dairy products that you can use to get your daily supply of milk.

DAIRY DICTIONARY

Dairy products include not only milk and cream, but also products such as butter, cheese, and frozen desserts. The following dictionary defines the dairy products you use, and offers buying and using tips where applicable.

MILK AND CREAM

MILK

Fresh Fluid Whole Milk

Fresh whole milk is usually homogenized and fortified with vitamins. Sometimes it's also fortified with minerals. It must meet the requirements for minimum milkfat content set by the State or municipality where it is sold. The milkfat content is usually about 3.25 percent, the minimum recommended by the Public Health Service "Grade A Pasteurized Milk Ordinance."

All Grade A milk and milk products sold today are pasteurized—heated to kill harmful bacteria. Grade A pasteurized milk, according to the standards recommended in the Pasteurized Milk Ordinance, must come from healthy cows and be produced, pasteurized, and handled under strict sanitary control enforced by State and local milk sanitation officials. Requirements may vary in different localities. The "Grade A" rating designates wholesomeness rather than a level of quality.

Homogenized milk has been treated to reduce the size of the milkfat globules. In homogenized milk, the cream does not separate and the product stays uniform throughout.

In Vitamin D milk, the vitamin D content has been increased to at least 400 U.S.P. units per quart. This is the minimum daily requirement for children, pregnant women, and nursing mothers.

Tips on Fresh Whole Milk:

• Get enough milk. Children under 9 need the equivalent of two to three 8-ounce glasses each day; children 9 to 12 and pregnant women need three or more; teenagers and nursing mothers need four or more; adults need two or more. See the Milk Equivalencies Chart on page seven to find out what foods can be substituted for fresh whole milk to meet these requirements.

Chocolate Flavored Milk and Chocolate Flavored Milk Drink

Chocolate flavored milk is made from pasteurized whole milk with sugar and chocolate sirup or cocoa added. In most States, regulations require that to be labeled chocolate flavored milk, the product must be made from whole milk; to be labeled chocolate flavored milk drink, it must be made from skim or partially skimmed milk.

Strawberry, coffee, or maple flavorings are sometimes used for other flavored milk and milk drinks.

Tips on Chocolate Flavored Milk:

• Chocolate flavored milk (or milk drink) can be heated for quick and easy hot chocolate.

• It can also be used in cookie or cake recipes that call for both milk and chocolate or cocoa.

Cultured Buttermilk

Cultured buttermilk is made by adding a lactic acid-producing bacterial culture to fresh pasteurized skim or partially skimmed milk. The resulting buttermilk is much thicker than skim milk with the same nutritive value. It has an acid flavor and it's a good thirst quencher. Almost all commercially marketed buttermilk is cultured. There is, however, a natural type which is a by-product of buttermaking.

Tips on Buttermilk:

●Always keep cultured buttermilk chilled. If allowed to warm, it may separate. If your buttermilk should separate, just stir it.

• Natural buttermilk is not sold in consumer packages. It's dried and used in pancake mixes and bakery products.

Dry Whole Milk

Dry whole milk is pasteurized whole milk with the water removed. It has only limited retail distribution. Where it is distributed, it's used mostly for infant feeding and by persons such as campers who don't have access to fresh milk. Dry whole milk is distributed mostly to manufacturers of chocolate and other candy.

Tip on Dry Whole Milk:

• Because of its fat content, dry whole milk doesn't keep as well as nonfat dry milk. If it is not used soon after the package is opened, it develops an off-flavor.

Nonfat Dry Milk

Nonfat dry milk is made by removing nearly all the fat and water from pasteurized milk. "Instant" nonfat dry milk is made of larger particles which are more easily dissolved in water. Nonfat dry milk has about half the calories of whole milk and the same nutritive value as fresh skim milk.

Some instant nonfat dry milk contains added vitamins A and D.

Tips on Nonfat Dry Milk:

• Nonfat dry milk needs no refrigeration and can be stored for several months in a cool dry place. After it is reconstituted, however, it should be refrigerated and handled like fresh milk.

• Nonfat dry milk can be used both as a beverage and in cooking. When using as a beverage, reconstitute it several hours before serving to allow time to chill. Use cool water.

• Nonfat dry milk is very economical. A family of four that has 21 quarts of whole milk delivered each week could save more than $3.00 each week by using nonfat dry milk instead.

Skim Milk

Fresh skim (or nonfat) milk usually has less than 0.5 percent milkfat, the percentage recommended to States under the Pasteurized Milk Ordinance. It is often fortified with vitamins A and D.

Tips on Skim Milk:

• Skim milk contains all the nutrients of whole milk except the fat.

• The flavor and food value of skim milk can be improved by adding a teaspoonful of instant nonfat dry milk to each glass.

Lowfat Milk

Lowfat milk usually has between 0.5 and 2 percent milkfat, depending on State regulations.

Tips on Lowfat Milk:

• This kind of milk may also be labeled "2%" or "2-10" milk in the store.

• Lowfat milk can be "made" at home by using half whole milk and half skim or instant nonfat dry milk.

Evaporated Milk

This type of milk is prepared by heating homogenized whole milk under a vacuum to remove half of its water, then sealing it in cans and sterilizing it. When mixed with an equal amount of water, its nutritive value is about the same as whole milk. Evaporated skim milk is also available.

Tips on Evaporated Milk:

• Refrigerate after opening.

• Evaporated milk is handy to store and is usually less expensive than fresh whole milk.

• A mixture of water and evaporated milk makes an inexpensive infant formula.

• Evaporated milk, with an equal amount of water added, may replace fresh milk in recipes. (Used full-strength, evaporated milk adds extra nutritive value.) It also can be used in coffee or on hot or cold cereal.

Sweetened Condensed Milk

Sweetened condensed milk is a concentrated milk with at least 40 percent sugar added to help preserve it. This canned milk is prepared by removing about half the water from whole milk. It is often used in candy and dessert recipes.

CREAM

The U.S. Food and Drug Administration has standards of identity for many of the different types of cream if they are shipped in interstate commerce. These standards give minimum milkfat requirements for each type of cream.

Light Cream (Coffee or Table Cream)

Light cream must have at least 18 percent milkfat according to Federal standards of identity and most State standards.

Tip on Light Cream:

• For maximum shelf life, do not return unused cream from a pitcher to its original container. Store it separately in the refrigerator, or better, pour only the amount to be used at one time.

Half-and-Half

Half-and-half is a mixture of milk and cream, homogenized. Under State requirements, it must have between 10 and 12 percent milkfat.

Tips on Half-and-Half:

• Half-and-half can be mixed at home using half homogenized whole milk and half table cream.

• As with light cream, do not return unused half-and-half to its original container.

Light Whipping Cream

Light whipping cream must have at least 30 percent milkfat under Federal standards of identity.

Tip on Light Whipping Cream:

• To whip this kind of cream, have both the bowl and the cream well chilled.

Heavy Whipping Cream

Heavy whipping cream must have at least 36 percent milkfat.

Tips on Heavy Whipping Cream:

• Although heavy whipping cream is more

easily whipped than light whipping cream, it is still good to have the cream and the bowl well chilled.

• Don't overwhip heavy cream. It may get grainy.

Sour Cream

Sour cream is made by adding lactic acid bacteria culture to light cream. It is smooth and thick and contains at least 18 percent milkfat.

Tips on Sour Cream:

• Sour cream is sometimes called "salad cream" or "cream dressing" in the supermarket.

• It's great on vegetables or baked potatoes.

Sour Half-and-Half

Sour half-and-half is the same as half-and-half except that a culture is added.

Tip on Sour Half-and-Half:

• This can replace sour cream, if you prefer less fat.

OTHER DAIRY PRODUCTS

BUTTER

Butter is made by churning pasteurized cream. It must have at least 80 percent milkfat, according to Federal law. Salt and coloring may be added. Whipped butter is regular butter that has been whipped for easier spreading. Whipping also increases the volume of butter.

Tips on Butter:

• Unsalted butter may be labeled **sweet butter** or **unsalted butter.** Some people prefer its flavor.

• Nothing beats butter for flavor in baking, or basting turkey or chicken.

• When using whipped butter in place of regular butter in recipes, use ⅓ to ½ more than the recipe calls for if the measurement is by volume (one cup, one half cup, etc.). If the measurement is by weight (¼ pound, ½ pound, etc), then use the same amount.

• Store butter in its original wrapping or container so it won't pick up odor from other foods.

• Butter can be kept frozen for up to a month.

• Butter is sold in 1-pound, ½-pound, and ¼-pound packages. It may be less expensive in the larger packages, and the reserve can be frozen.

• For easier spreading, let butter warm to room temperature. (This isn't necessary for whipped butter.)

• Make butter the first ingredient on sandwiches. It adds moisture and flavor and keeps the filling from soaking into the bread.

CHEESE

Natural cheese is cheese made directly from milk. There are virtually hundreds of varieties of natural cheese.

Process cheese is a blend of natural cheeses which have been shredded, mixed, and heated. This cheese may contain pimentos, fruits, vegetables, or meats.

If the label says "process cheese food," other ingredients such as nonfat dry milk have been mixed in.

"Process cheese spread" has higher moisture content and lower milkfat content than process cheese and cheese food. It's more spreadable.

Process cheese products usually come packed in slices, loaves, and jars.

Cottage cheese is a soft unripened natural

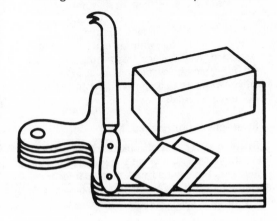

cheese that can be bought in cup-shaped containers or tumblers. It may be bought plain or creamed and in different curd sizes. Federal standards require that it have no more than 80 percent moisture. Creamed cottage cheese contains a minimum of 4 percent fat. Cottage cheese should be used within a few days of purchase.

Tip on Cheese:

Cheese has a high food value and comes in a wide variety of flavors to suit every taste. For complete details on the great variety of cheeses available, see "How to Buy Cheese," pages 8-18.

YOGURT

Yogurt is a custard-like product made by fermenting milk with a special culture. It is usually made from homogenized, pasteurized whole milk, but may be made from skim or partly skimmed milk. Yogurt has the same nutritive value as the milk from which it is made. Often yogurt is sweetened and fruit flavored.

Tips on Yogurt:

Yogurt can be served at any meal or as a snack. A fruit-flavored yogurt is good for breakfast, or for dessert.
• Yogurt should be kept cold, but not frozen. If allowed to warm to room temperature, it might separate slightly.

FROZEN DESSERTS

Frozen desserts include ice cream, ice milk, sherbets, and ices in their various forms (cartoned, cones, popsicles, etc.) If they are shipped in interstate commerce, they must meet U.S. Food and Drug Administration standards of identity. In addition, the U.S. Department of Agriculture has issued recommended standards for the manufacture of frozen desserts. These can be adopted voluntarily by any State. They set minimum quality requirements for the product as well as for its dairy ingredients. The standards also provide criteria for plant sanitation.

Ice Cream

Ice cream is made from cream, milk, sugar, flavorings, and stabilizers. It must contain at least 10 percent milkfat.

Tips on Ice Cream:

• Keep ice cream in a tightly closed carton and try to use it within a week if you store it in your refrigerator frozen food compartment. If you store it in a deep freezer, it will keep for a month or two (so long as the temperature is kept below zero). It should be kept hard frozen to prevent it from becoming "icy."

Ice cream is easier to serve if it is transferred from the frozen food compartment to the refrigerator section a short time before serving—about 10 minutes for a pint and 20 minutes for a half gallon.

Frozen Custard (French Ice Cream)

Some ice cream has egg yolks added. This may be called frozen custard, French ice cream, or New York ice cream.

Ice Milk

Ice milk is made from milk, stabilizers, sugar, and flavorings. It must contain between 2 and 7 percent milkfat if it is sold in interstate commerce. The soft-serve frozen dessert you can buy at the roadside stand is like ice milk except that it's specially processed to be served soft.

Tip on Ice Milk:

● Treat ice milk as you do ice cream. (See "Tips for Ice Cream.")

Sherbet

Sherbet is made from milk, fruit or fruit juice, stabilizers, and sugars. Sherbet has a high level of sugar—about twice as much as ice cream. It must have 1 to 2 percent milkfat.

Tip on Sherbet:

● Handle sherbet like ice cream. (See "Tips for Ice Cream.")

Water Ice

Water ice is like sherbet except that it contains no milk solids.

MARKS OF QUALITY

To help you buy dairy products, the U.S. Department of Agriculture has quality grades, or a "Quality Approved" rating, for manufactured dairy products. For a manufacturer to use the USDA grade or "Quality Approved" shield on his product lábels, his plant must meet USDA's specifications and must operate under the continuous inspection of USDA's Agricultural Marketing Service.

To qualify, a plant must pass an initial survey by a USDA dairy inspector and subsequent inspections made a number of times a year. The inspector checks the plant and surrounding areas to see if they are clean, orderly, soundly constructed, and in good repair. Processing and packaging techniques must be sanitary. Incoming raw products are checked regularly, and the plant must have a laboratory testing program to maintain proper quality control. Even the labels must be approved by USDA before the packages can carry the shield. The labels may carry no conflicting or misleading statements.

During processing, a USDA inspector keeps constant check on all aspects of product quality, right down to a final check on the product in consumer packages. Some brands of the following products bear a USDA shield.

COTTAGE CHEESE AND PASTEURIZED PROCESS CHEESE

Cottage cheese and pasteurized process cheese may bear the USDA "Quality Approved" shield if they are of good quality and are made under USDA supervision.

BUTTER

One way to be assured of high quality butter is to look for the USDA grade shield on the package. The grade shield (AA, A, or B) means that the butter has been tested and graded by experienced government graders. Butter graders judge quality by U.S. grade standards that set forth the requirements for each grade. They also test the keeping quality of butter.

U.S. Grade AA Butter:

● has delicate sweet flavor, with a fine highly pleasing aroma;

● is made from high-quality fresh sweet cream;

● has a smooth, creamy texture with good spreadability;

● has salt completely dissolved and blended in just the right amount.

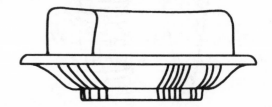

U.S. Grade A Butter

- has a pleasing flavor;
- is made from fresh cream;
- is fairly smooth in texture;
- rates close to the top grade.

U.S. Grade B Butter:

- may have a slightly acid flavor;
- generally is made from selected sour cream;
- is readily acceptable to many consumers.

CHEDDAR CHEESE

USDA Grades AA and A are used on Cheddar cheese. As with butter, U.S. Grade AA is the best and Grade A is almost as good. For more on Cheddar cheese grades, see "How to Buy Cheese," pages 8-18.

INSTANT NONFAT DRY MILK

To earn the "U.S. Extra Grade" shield, instant nonfat dry milk must have a sweet and pleasing flavor and a natural color. It must also dissolve immediately when mixed with water.

MILK EQUIVALENCIES

On the basis of the calcium they provide, the following are alternatives for 1 cup of fresh whole milk:

1⅓ ounces natural Cheddar cheese

1½ ounces process Cheddar cheese

1⅓ cups creamed cottage cheese

1 cup cocoa made with milk

1 cup custard

1⅓ cups ice cream

1 cup ice milk, soft serve

¾ cup   homemade macaroni and cheese

1 milkshake (made with ⅔ cup milk and ½ cup ice cream)

1 cup oyster stew

⅛ of 15-inch-diameter round pizza, made with cheese topping

1 cup pudding, made with milk and cornstarch

1⅓ cups canned cream soup, prepared with equal volume of milk

1 cup yogurt

How to Buy CHEESE

By F. E. Fenton, Chief, Standardization Branch
Dairy Division
Agricultural Marketing Service

Many countries have developed one or more varieties of cheese peculiar to their own conditions and culture.

When the colonists settled in the New World they brought with them their own methods of making their favorite kind of cheese. The first Cheddar cheese factory in the United States was built by Jesse Williams, near Rome, Oneida County, N.Y., in 1851. As the population increased in the East, and there was a corresponding increase in the demand for market milk, the cheese industry gradually moved westward. Cheesemaking in the United States and in the other leading cheese-producing countries of the world is now largely a factory industry.

Many of the popular varieties, although originating in Europe, are now produced in the United States and are available in most food stores, delicatessens and specialty cheese stores.

MAKING NATURAL CHEESE

The making of natural cheese is an art centuries old. It consists of separating most of the milk solids from the milk by curdling with rennet or bacterial culture or both and separating the curd from the whey by heating, stirring, and pressing. Most cheeses in this country are made from whole milk. For certain types of cheese both milk and cream are used and for other types, skim milk, whey or mixtures of all of these are used.

The distinctive flavor and body and texture characteristics of the various cheeses are due to: (1) the kind of milk used, (2) the method used for curdling the milk and for cutting, cooking, and forming the curd, (3) the type of bacteria or molds used in ripening, (4) the amount of salt or other seasonings added and (5) the conditions of ripening such as temperature, humidity and length of time. Sometimes only minor differences in the procedures followed may make the difference between one variety of cheese and another.

After the cheese has been formed into its characteristic shape it is given a coating of wax or other protective coating or wrapping and allowed to cure or age for varying lengths of time depending upon the kind or variety of cheese being made.

When the cheese has reached its proper curing stage it is often cut or sliced from larger blocks or wheels into more suitable sizes for consumer use. The refrigerated showcase in a modern food market is most enticing with its display of various shapes and sizes of cheese packages such as wedges, oblongs, segments, cubes, slices, blocks and cut portions.

CARE IN THE HOME

All natural cheese should be kept refrigerated. Soft unripened cheeses, such as cottage, cream or Neufchatel, are quite perishable and should be used within a few days after purchase. Ripened or cured cheeses keep well in the refrigerator for several weeks if protected from mold contamination and drying out. When possible the original wrapper or covering should be left on the cheese. The cut surface of cheese should be covered with wax paper, foil, or plastic wrapping material to protect the surface from drying. If large pieces are to be stored for any extended length of time, the cut surface may be dipped in hot paraffin. Small pieces may be completely rewrapped. Mold which may develop on natural cheeses is not harmful, and it is easily scraped or cut from the surface of the cheese. The particular mold in the interior of such cheeses as Blue, Gorgonzola, Roquefort or Stilton has been carefully developed to produce the characteristic color and distinctive flavor of those varieties and is consumed as part of the cheese.

Ends or pieces of cheese that have become dried out and hard may be grated and kept refrigerated in a clean, tightly covered glass jar, and used for garnishing or accenting.

Cheese with an aromatic or a strong odor such as Limburger should be stored in a tightly covered jar or container. Such cheeses are fast curing and are best when used within a reasonable time after purchase.

Normally cheese should not be allowed to freeze as this may damage the characteristic body and texture and cause the cheese to become crumbly and mealy. However, small pieces (1 pound or less) not over 1 inch thick of certain varieties may be frozen satisfactorily for as long as 6 months if handled and stored properly. Since it is necessary that the cheese be frozen quickly, the temperature of the freezer should be 0° F. or lower. Cut cheese should be carefully wrapped (foil or other moistureproof freezer wrapping should be pressed tightly against surfaces to eliminate air, and to prevent evaporation), then frozen immediately. Among the varieties of cheese which can be successfully frozen in small pieces are: Brick, Cheddar, Edam, Gouda, Muenster, Port du Salut, Swiss, Provolone, Mozzarella, and Camembert. Small sizes as in the case of Camembert can be frozen in their original package. When removed from the freezer, cheese should be thawed in the refrigerator and used as soon as possible after thawing.

Except for soft unripened cheeses such as cottage and cream cheese, all cheese should be served unchilled in order to help bring out its distinctive flavor and texture characteristics. This usually requires 20 minutes to 1 hour or more at room temperature.

USES

Cheese is one of the most nutritious and versatile foods. Because it is an excellent source of many important nutrients in the diet and because it is a well-liked food, cheese is used freely by nutritionists and homemakers in planning meals and in the preparation of many flavorful dishes. With the wide variety of flavors, colors, and consistencies to choose from, natural cheeses are suitable for any meal of the day, from appetizers to desserts, and between-meal snacks as well. Whether served separately or in combination dishes, cheese adds zest and flavor to other foods. There is a cheese to suit every taste, mood or occasion.

Some of the many ways of using different kinds of cheese are as follows:

(a) Main dish in the form of fondue, soufflé, Welsh rabbit, omelet, pizza, or in combination with potatoes, other vegetables, rice, macaroni, noodles or spaghetti.

(b) Salads and salad dressings.

(c) Assorted cheeses on trays with fruit, nuts and crackers or chips.

(d) Appetizers in the form of cut cheese or as spreads and dips.

(e) Sliced in toasted or cold sandwiches or as an ingredient in sandwich spreads and sauces.

(f) Grated as a garnish for soups, sauces and hot dishes.

(g) Desserts, as cheese and crackers, cheese cakes, cheese pies, or fruit pies with cheese.

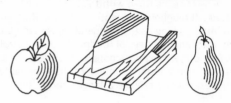

RIPENING CLASSIFICATIONS

Unripened

The soft unripened varieties such as cottage cheese contain relatively high moisture and do not undergo any curing or ripening. They are consumed fresh—soon after manufacture. The firm unripened cheeses such as Gjetost and Mysost also may be used soon after manufacture but because they contain very low moisture may be kept for several weeks or months.

Soft Ripened

In the soft ripened cheeses, curing progresses from the outside or rind of the cheese, towards the center. Particular molds or culture of bacteria or both, which grow on the surface of the cheese aid in developing the characteristic flavor and body and texture during the curing process. Curing continues as long as the temperature is favorable. These cheeses usually contain more moisture than semi-soft ripened varieties.

Semisoft Ripened

Unlike the soft ripened varieties, these cheeses ripen from the interior as well as from the surface. This ripening process begins soon after the cheese is formed, with the aid of a characteristic bacterial or mold culture or both. Curing continues as long as the temperature is favorable. These cheeses contain higher moisture than the firm ripened varieties.

Firm Ripened

These cheeses ripen with the aid of a bacterial culture, throughout the entire cheese. Ripening continues as long as the temperature is favorable. The rate and degree of curing is also closely related to the moisture content. Therefore, these cheeses, being lower in moisture than the softer varieties, usually require a longer curing time.

Very Hard Ripened

These cheeses also are cured with the aid of a bacterial culture and enzymes. The rate of curing however is much slower because of the very low moisture and higher salt content.

Blue-Vein Mold Ripened

Curing is accomplished by the aid of bacteria but more particularly by the use of a characteristic mold culture that grows throughout the interior of the cheese to produce the familiar appearance and characteristic flavor.

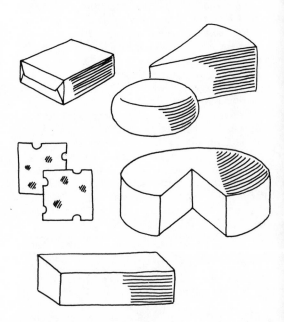

KINDS OF CHEESE

The charts in this pamphlet will help you in learning some of the more popular and generally available varieties of natural cheese, their general classification, principal characteristics, and some of their uses.

CHARACTERISTICS OF SOME POPULAR VARIETIES OF NATURAL CHEESES

Kind or name Place of origin	Kind of milk used in manufacture	Ripening or curing time	Flavor	Body and texture	Color	Retail packaging	Uses
			SOFT, UNRIPENED VARIETIES				
Cottage, plain or creamed. (Unknown)	Cow's milk skimmed; plain curd, or plain curd with cream added.	Unripened	Mild, acid	Soft, curd particles of varying size.	White to creamy white.	Cup-shaped containers, tumblers, dishes.	Salads, with fruits, vegetables, sandwiches, dips, cheese cake.
Cream, plain (U.S.A.)	Cream from cow's milk.	Unripened	Mild, acid	Soft and smooth	White	3- to 8-oz. packages	Salads, dips, sandwiches, snacks, cheese cake, desserts.
Neufchatel (Nū̇-shä-tel'). (France)	Cow's milk	Unripened	Mild, acid	Soft, smooth similar to cream cheese but lower in milkfat.	White	4- to 8-oz. packages.	Salads, dips, sandwiches, snacks, cheese cake, desserts.
Ricotta (Rĭ-cŏ'-ta) (Italy)	Cow's milk, whole or partly skimmed, or whey from cow's milk with whole or skim milk added. In Italy, whey from sheep's milk.	Unripened	Sweet, nutlike.	Soft, moist or dry	White	Pint and quart paper and plastic containers, 3 lb. metal cans.	Appetizers, salads, snacks, lasagne, ravioli, noodles and other cooked dishes, grating, desserts.
			FIRM, UNRIPENED VARIETIES				
Gjetost,[1] (Yet'ŏst). (Norway)	Whey from goat's milk or a mixture of whey from goat's and cow's milk.	Unripened	Sweetish, caramel.	Firm, buttery consistency.	Golden brown	Cubical and rectangular.	Snacks, desserts, served with dark breads, crackers, biscuits or muffins.
Mysost (Müs-ôst) also called Primost (Prēm'-ôst). (Norway)	Whey from cow's milk.	Unripened	Sweetish, caramel.	Firm, buttery consistency.	Light brown	Cubical, cylindrical, pie-shaped wedges.	Snacks, desserts, served with dark breads.
Mozzarella (Mŏ-tsa-rel'la) also called Scamorza. (Italy)	Whole or partly skimmed cow's milk. In Italy, originally made from buffalo's milk.	Unripened	Delicate, mild.	Slightly firm, plastic.	Creamy white	Small round or braided form, shredded, sliced.	Snacks, toasted sandwiches, cheeseburgers, cooking, as in meat loaf, or topping for lasagne, pizza, and casseroles.

[1] Imported only.

CHARACTERISTICS OF SOME POPULAR VARIETIES OF NATURAL CHEESES—Continued

Kind or name Place of origin	Kind of milk used in manufacture	Ripening or curing time	Flavor	Body and texture	Color	Retail packaging	Uses
SOFT, RIPENED VARIETIES							
Brie (Brē) (France)	Cow's milk.........	4 to 8 weeks.	Mild to pungent.	Soft, smooth when ripened.	Creamy yellow interior; edible thin brown and white crust.	Circular, pie-shaped wedges.	Appetizers, sandwiches, snacks, good with crackers and fruit, dessert.
Camembert (Kăm′ĕm-bâr). (France)	Cow's milk.........	4 to 8 weeks.	Mild to pungent.	Soft, smooth; very soft when fully ripened.	Creamy yellow interior; edible thin white, or gray-white crust.	Small circular cakes and pie-shaped portions.	Appetizers, sandwiches, snacks, good with crackers and fruit such as pears and apples, dessert.
Limburger (Belgium)	Cow's milk.........	4 to 8 weeks.	Highly pungent, very strong.	Soft, smooth when ripened; usually contains small irregular openings.	Creamy white interior; reddish yellow surface.	Cubical, rectangular.	Appetizers, snacks, good with crackers, rye or other dark breads, dessert.
SEMISOFT, RIPENED VARIETIES							
Bel Paese [2] (Bĕl Pä-ä-zē). (Italy)	Cow's milk.........	6 to 8 weeks.	Mild to moderately robust.	Soft to medium firm, creamy.	Creamy yellow interior; slightly gray or brownish surface sometimes covered with yellow wax coating.	Small wheels, wedges, segments.	Appetizers, good with crackers, snacks, sandwiches, dessert.
(Brick) (U.S.A.)	Cow's milk.........	2 to 4 months.	Mild to moderately sharp.	Semisoft to medium firm, elastic, numerous small mechanical openings.	Creamy yellow....	Loaf, brick, slices, cut portions.	Appetizers, sandwiches, snacks, dessert.
Muenster (Mün′ stêr). (Germany)	Cow's milk.........	1 to 8 weeks.	Mild to mellow.	Semisoft, numerous small mechanical openings. Contains more moisture than brick.	Creamy white interior; yellow tan surface.	Circular cake, blocks, wedges, segments, slices.	Appetizers, sandwiches, snacks, dessert.
Port du Salut (Pōr dü Sà-lü′). (France)	Cow's milk.........	6 to 8 weeks.	Mellow to robust.	Semisoft, smooth, buttery, small openings.	Creamy yellow....	Wheels and wedges.	Appetizers, snacks, served with raw fruit, dessert.

[2] Italian trademark—licensed for manufacture in U.S.A.; also imported.

CHARACTERISTICS OF SOME POPULAR VARIETIES OF NATURAL CHEESES—Continued

Kind or name Place of origin	Kind of milk used in manufacture	Ripening or curing time	Flavor	Body and texture	Color	Retail packaging	Uses
FIRM RIPENED VARIETIES							
Cheddar (England)	Cow's milk	1 to 12 months or more.	Mild to very sharp.	Firm, smooth, some mechanical openings.	White to medium-yellow-orange.	Circular, cylindrical loaf, pie-shaped wedges, oblongs, slices, cubes, shredded, grated.	Appetizers, sandwiches, sauces, on vegetables, in hot dishes, toasted sandwiches, grating, cheeseburgers, dessert.
Colby (U.S.A.)	Cow's milk	1 to 3 months.	Mild to mellow.	Softer and more open than Cheddar.	White to medium-yellow-orange.	Cylindrical, pie-shaped wedges.	Sandwiches, snacks cheeseburgers.
Caciocavallo (Kä'chō-kä-val'lō) (Italy)	Cow's milk. In Italy, cow's milk or mixtures of sheep's, goat's, and cow's milk.	3 to 12 months.	Piquant, similar to Provolone but not smoked.	Firm, lower in milkfat and moisture than Provolone.	Light or white interior; clay or tan colored surface.	Spindle or ten-pin shaped, bound with cord, cut pieces.	Snacks, sandwiches, cooking, dessert; suitable for grating after prolonged curing.
Edam (Ē'dăm) (Netherlands)	Cow's milk, partly skimmed.	2 to 3 months.	Mellow, nut-like.	Semisoft to firm, smooth; small irregularly shaped or round holes; lower milkfat than Gouda.	Creamy yellow or medium yellow-orange interior; surface coated with red wax.	Cannon ball shaped loaf, cut pieces, oblongs.	Appetizers, snacks, salads, sandwiches, seafood sauces, dessert.
FIRM RIPENED VARIETIES: Continued							
Gouda (Gou'-dä) (Netherlands)	Cow's milk, whole or partly skimmed.	2 to 6 months.	Mellow, nut-like.	Semisoft to firm, smooth; small irregularly shaped or round holes; higher milkfat than Edam.	Creamy yellow or medium yellow-orange; may or may not have red wax coating.	Ball shaped with flattened top and bottom.	Appetizers, snacks, salads, sandwiches, seafood sauces, dessert.
Provolone (Prō-vō-lō'-ne) also smaller sizes and shapes called Provolette, Provoloncini. (Italy)	Cow's milk	2 to 12 months or more	Mellow to sharp, smoky, salty.	Firm, smooth.	Light creamy interior; light brown or golden yellow surface.	Pear shaped, sausage and salami shaped, wedges, slices.	Appetizers, sandwiches, snacks, souffle, macaroni and spaghetti dishes, pizza, suitable for grating when fully cured and dried.
Swiss, also called Emmentaler. (Switzerland)	Cow's milk	3 to 9 months.	Sweet, nut-like.	Firm, smooth with large round eyes.	Light yellow.	Segments, pieces, slices.	Sandwiches, snacks, sauces, fondue, cheeseburgers.

CHARACTERISTICS OF SOME POPULAR VARIETIES OF NATURAL CHEESES—Continued

Kind or name / Place of origin	Kind of milk used in manufacture	Ripening or curing time	Flavor	Body and texture	Color	Retail packaging	Uses
VERY HARD RIPENED VARIETIES							
Parmesan (Pär´mē-zän) also called Reggiano. (Italy)	Partly skimmed cow's milk.	14 months to 2 years.	Sharp, piquant.	Very hard, granular, lower moisture and milkfat than Romano.	Creamy white.	Cylindrical, wedges, shredded, grated.	Grated for seasoning in soups, or vegetables, spaghetti, ravioli, breads, popcorn, used extensively in pizza and lasagne.
Romano (Rō-mā´nō) also called Sardo Romano Pecorino Romano. (Italy)	Cow's milk. In Italy, sheep's milk (Italian law).	5 to 12 months.	Sharp, piquant.	Very hard granular.	Yellowish-white interior, greenish-black surface.	Round with flat ends, wedges, shredded, grated.	Seasoning in soups, casserole dishes, ravioli, sauces, breads, suitable for grating when cured for about one year.
Sap Sago [1] (Săp´să-gō). (Switzerland)	Skimmed cow's milk.	5 months or more.	Sharp, pungent clover-like.	Very hard.	Light green by addition of dried, powdered clover leaves.	Conical, shakers.	Grated to flavor soups, meats, macaroni, spaghetti, hot vegetables; mixed with butter makes a good spread on crackers or bread.
BLUE-VEIN MOLD RIPENED VARIETIES							
Blue, spelled Bleu on imported cheese. (France)	Cow's milk.	2 to 6 months.	Tangy, peppery.	Semisoft, pasty, sometimes crumbly.	White interior, marbled or streaked with blue veins of mold.	Cylindrical, wedges, oblongs, squares, cut portions.	Appetizers, salads, dips, salad dressing, sandwich spreads, good with crackers, dessert.
Gorgonzola (Gôr-gŏn-zō´-iä). (Italy)	Cow's milk. In Italy, cow's milk or goat's milk or mixtures of these.	3 to 12 months.	Tangy, peppery.	Semisoft, pasty, sometimes crumbly, lower moisture than Blue.	Creamy white interior, mottled or streaked with blue-green veins of mold. Clay colored surface.	Cylindrical, wedges, oblongs.	Appetizers, snacks, salads, dips, sandwich spread, good with crackers, dessert.
Roquefort [1] (Rŏk´-fĕrt) or (Rŏk.fôr´). (France).	Sheep's milk.	2 to 5 months or more.	Sharp, slightly peppery.	Semisoft, pasty, sometimes crumbly.	White or creamy white interior, marbled or streaked with blue veins of mold.	Cylindrical, wedges.	Appetizers, snacks, salads, dips, sandwich spreads, good with crackers, dessert.
Stilton [1] (England).	Cow's milk.	2 to 6 months.	Piquant, milder than Gorgonzola or Roquefort.	Semisoft, flaky; slightly more crumbly than Blue.	Creamy white interior, marbled or streaked with blue-green veins of mold.	Circular, wedges, oblongs.	Appetizers, snacks, salads, dessert.

[1] Imported only.

MEET THE FAVORITE AMERICAN-MADE CHEESES

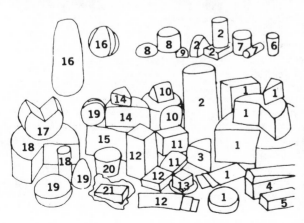

1. Cheddar
2. Colby
3. Monterey or Jack
4. Pasteurized Process Cheese
5. Cheese Foods
6. Cheese Spreads
7. Cold Pack Cheese Food or
   Club Cheese
8. Gouda and Edam
9. Camembert
10. Muenster
11. Brick
12. Swiss
13. Limburger
14. Blue
15. Gorgonzola
16. Provolone
17. Romano
18. Parmesan
19. Mozzarella and Scamorze
20. Cottage Cheese
21. Cream Cheese

PASTEURIZED PROCESS CHEESE

Pasteurized process cheese is a blend of fresh and aged natural cheeses which have been shredded, mixed and heated (pasteurized), after which no further ripening occurs. It melts easily when reheated. The blend may consist of one or two or more varieties of natural cheese and may contain pimentos, fruits, vegetables, or meats. Smoked cheese or smoke flavor may also be added.

The flavor of pasteurized process cheese depends largely upon the flavor of the cheese used which may be modified by flavoring materials added. Pasteurized Gruyere cheese has a nut-sweet flavor, somewhat similar to Swiss.

Some other available varieties are: pasteurized process American cheese, pasteurized process Swiss cheese, pasteurized process Swiss cheese blended with American, and pasteurized process Brick cheese.

Process cheese is packaged in slices, ½-, 1- and 2-pound loaves and cut portions.

It may be used in main dishes, for snacks and cheeseburgers, with cold cuts and salads, on grilled or toasted sandwiches, in numerous sandwich combinations and in casseroles.

PASTEURIZED PROCESS CHEESE FOOD

Pasteurized process cheese food is prepared in much the same manner as process cheese except that it contains less cheese, with nonfat dry milk, or whey solids and water added. This results in a lower milk fat content and more moisture than in process cheese. Pasteurized process cheese food also may contain pimentos, fruits, vegetables or meats or may have a smoked flavor.

Cheese food is milder in flavor, has a softer texture, spreads more easily and melts quicker than process cheese due to the higher moisture. The most popular variety is pasteurized process American cheese food and is packaged in slices, rolls, links and loaves.

It may be used in any place where process cheese is used though it is not likely to add as much cheese flavor.

PASTEURIZED PROCESS CHEESE SPREAD

Pasteurized process cheese spread is made in much the same manner as pasteurized process cheese food but generally contains higher moisture, and the milk fat content is usually lower. A stabilizer is used in the preparation of this product to prevent separation of ingredients. It is normally more spreadable than cheese food. Cheese spread also may contain pimentos, fruits, vegetables or meats or may have a smoked flavor.

The flavor of pasteurized process cheese spread depends largely upon the flavor of the cheese used which may be modified by flavoring materials added.

Some available varieties are: pasteurized process American cheese spread, pasteurized process pimento cheese spread, pasteurized process pineapple cheese spread and pasteurized process Blue cheese spread.

Spreads are packaged in jars and loaves convenient for use as snacks, in stuffing celery stalks, and in deviled eggs, noodle casseroles, meat balls, hot vegetables, sandwiches, sauces, and dressings.

COLDPACK CHEESE

Coldpack cheese or Club cheese is a blend of the same or two or more varieties of fresh and aged natural cheese, as in process cheese, except that the cheese is mixed into a uniform product without heating. It may have a smoked flavor.

The principal varieties are coldpack American cheese and cold pack Swiss cheese.

The flavor is the same as the natural cheese used and usually is aged or sharp. The body is softer than the natural cheese and it spreads easily.

Coldpack cheese is packed in jars, rolls, or links and it is especially good as an appetizer, snack, or dessert.

COLDPACK CHEESE FOOD

Coldpack cheese food is prepared in the same manner as Coldpack cheese but includes other dairy ingredients as used in process cheese food. In addition, sweetening agents such as sugar and corn sirup may be added.

Coldpack cheese food may contain pimentos, fruits, vegetables or meats or may have a smoked flavor.

The flavor resembles the cheese from which it is made but is milder. It is softer than the natural cheese and spreads more easily due to the other ingredients added and the higher moisture content.

It is packaged in the same way as Coldpack cheese and may be served in the same manner.

BUYING CHEESE

CHECK THE LABEL

The labels of natural cheese, pasteurized process cheese, and related products carry important descriptive information. The name of a natural cheese will appear as the variety such as "Cheddar cheese", "Swiss cheese", or "Blue cheese."

Pasteurized process cheese labels will always include the words "pasteurized process", together with the name of the variety or varieties of cheese used, for instance, "pasteurized process American cheese" or "pasteurized process Swiss and American cheese".

Cheese food also contains ingredients other than cheese and therefore is labeled as "pasteurized process cheese food". Cheese spreads have a different composition from cheese foods and

are labeled as "pasteurized process cheese spread". All the ingredients used in the preparation of these products are listed on the respective label along with the kinds or varieties of cheese used in the mixture. Also the milkfat and moisture content may be shown.

Coldpack cheese and coldpack cheese food are labeled in the same manner as other cheese and cheese foods except that "club cheese" or "comminuted cheese" may be substituted for the name "coldpack cheese".

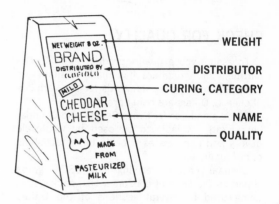

CHECK THE CURE

A very important bit of information on the label of certain varieties of natural cheese pertains to the age or degree of curing. For instance, Cheddar cheese may be labeled as "mild", "medium" or "mellow", or "aged" or "sharp". In some cases pasteurized process cheese may be labeled to indicate a sharp flavor when a much higher proportion of sharp or aged cheese was used in its preparation.

CHECK THE NAME

Look for the name of the article. Do not confuse the brand name with the name of the cheese. For some purposes you may want natural cheese, for others, process cheese or cheese food, and for still others, pasteurized process cheese spread or coldpack cheese may best serve your needs. In many cases they may be packaged alike but the names on the labels will be different.

CHECK FOR QUALITY

To assure you a quality product the U.S. Department of Agriculture has made available to manufacturers quality standards for two varieties of cheese. Others are being prepared.

Grade standards for Swiss Cheese and Cheddar cheese are available to be used by wholesale buyers and handlers as a basis for establishing price/quality terms.

Cheddar cheese carrying the USDA grade shield on the label of consumer-size packages is being used in several sections of the United States.

The USDA grade shield means that the Cheddar cheese has been inspected and graded by an experienced and highly trained Government grader. And it means the cheese was produced in a USDA inspected and approved plant, under sanitary conditions. It is your guarantee of consistent and dependable quality.

Cheddar cheese carrying the U.S. Grade AA shield is the highest quality. It meets exacting USDA standards, has a fine, highly pleasing Cheddar flavor, a smooth compact texture, uniform color, and attractive appearance.

To earn this grade, cheese must be produced with special care—in the quality of the milk, cheese-making skill, curing or ripening process, and packaging.

The AA shield is assurance of consistently fine Cheddar flavor and texture in every package.

Cheddar cheese bearing the U.S. Grade A shield on the package is also of good quality—but not as high as AA. The flavor is pleasing; however, there may be more variation in flavor and texture between packages. Cheese and cheese products not covered by a U.S. grade standard may be inspected and bear the USDA "Quality Approved" inspection shield on the container. Pasteurized Process Cheese, Cheese Food and Spreads, and Cottage cheese are current examples of cheese products being inspected by the U.S. Department of Agriculture.

To carry the "Quality Approved" shield, the product must be manufactured in a plant meeting the USDA sanitary specifications for plant and equipment as well as the quality specifications for the cheese itself.

How to Buy EGGS

LOOK FOR THE USDA SHIELD—

● It can tell you:

● You can find it on:

grade (quality) ►

and size ►

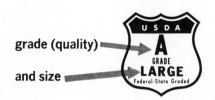

the carton
or on a
tape sealing
the carton

The official grade shield certifies that the eggs have been graded for quality and size under Federal-State supervision. The grading service is provided on a voluntary basis to those who request and pay a fee for it.

Weighing for size

Mass candling for quality check

Checking quality by instrument

SELECT BY GRADE (QUALITY)

GRADE refers to interior quality (see broken out appearance below) and condition and appearance of shell.

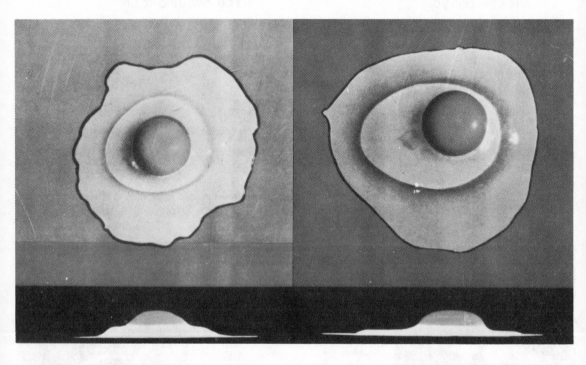

Grade AA (or Fresh Fancy) egg covers small area; white is thick, stands high; yolk is firm and high.

Grade A egg covers moderate area; white is reasonably thick, stands fairly high; yolk is firm and high.

The three consumer grades are U.S. Grade AA (or Fresh Fancy), A, and B.
Fresh Fancy Quality (or Grade AA) eggs are produced under USDA's Quality Control Program. These eggs reach the market quickly under strictly controlled conditions, guaranteeing the consumer a fresh, top-quality product.

The higher quality eggs (AA or Fresh Fancy, and A) are ideal for ALL purposes, but are especially good for frying and poaching where appearance is important.

Grade B eggs are good for general cooking and baking where appearance is not important.

SELECT BY SIZE (Weight Classes)

SIZE refers to minimum weight per dozen.

The size may be shown within the grade shield or elsewhere on the carton.

Size and quality are not related — they are entirely different.

For example, large eggs may be of high or low quality; high quality eggs may be either large or small.

The sizes most often found are:

	Minimum Weight per Dozen
Extra Large	27 oz.
Large	24 oz.
Medium	21 oz.

Other sizes sometimes available are:

	Minimum Weight per Dozen
Jumbo	30 oz.
Small	18 oz.
Peewee	15 oz.

EXTRA LARGE
27 OZ. PER DOZEN
LARGE
24 OZ. PER DOZEN
MEDIUM
21 OZ. PER DOZEN

SIZE AND PRICE

● EGG PRICES vary by size for the same grade. The amount of price variation depends on the supply of the various sizes.

● Generally speaking, if there is less than a 7 cent price spread per dozen eggs between one size and the next smaller size in the same grade, you will get more for your money by buying the larger size.

● When Large eggs sell for 60 cents per dozen, that's the equivalent of 40 cents per pound — very reasonable for a pound of high protein food.

EGG TIPS

● Buy eggs from a refrigerated case.

● Refrigerate eggs promptly at home, large end up, to help maintain quality.

● Variations in temperature while the eggs are stored cause egg whites to become thin.

● Use only high-quality, clean eggs with sound shells when making egg nogs, milk shakes, or lightly cooked dishes.

● Cook at low to moderate temperatures — high temperatures and over-cooking toughen eggs.

● Eggs are nutritious! They contain significant amounts of vitamin A, iron, protein, and riboflavin (vitamin B_2), as well as smaller amounts of many other nutrients.

● The thick, white, cord-like material located on opposite sides of the yolk is called the chalaza and is a normal part of the egg. The chalaza holds the yolk in place in the white.

● Shell color is determined by breed of the hen and does not affect the grade, nutritive value, flavor, or cooking performance of the egg.

● Egg protein is so near perfection that scientists often use it as a standard to measure the value of protein in other foods.

● Eggs are an important, easily and completely digested food for all ages — from infancy to old age.

● Eggs are versatile — serve them often — "as is" or in combination with other foods.

How to Buy DRY BEANS, PEAS, and LENTILS

Dry beans, peas, and lentils—delicious, nutritious, low-cost foods that can be served in so many ways. But how much do you **really** know about these foods? For example, what is a lentil? What is the difference between black-eye peas and black-eye beans? What quality factors should you bear in mind when buying beans, peas, and lentils? How do you store and prepare them? Which need soaking and which do not before cooking? What are the varieties of beans and peas available? These are some of the factors a smart shopper should consider when buying these products.

Dry beans, and their close cousins, dry peas and lentils, are food bargains. They are an excellent source of protein—in fact, dry beans provide more protein for your money than most other foods. And the protein derived from these foods, when combined with protein from meats and other foods of animal origin, makes an unbeatable "protein team" which the body needs to build and repair vital organs and tissues.

Dry beans, peas, and lentils provide a wealth of energy and nutrition at a cost per pound that is nominal. They contain B vitamins, such as thiamin, and riboflavin, and some are a good source of calcium. They are real nuggets of mineral value for the iron they provide—a ¾ cup serving of dried beans or dry peas, for example, provides about a third of the iron recommended daily for an adult male.

The dry bean sometimes is considered a building food, an energy food, and to some extent a protective food. Peas and lentils also fall into these same categories, and since their fat content is low they are useful in some special diets.

A cup of cooked dried red beans provides about 230 calories and the following percentages of the minimum daily recommended allowances for adults:

Nutrient	Women (22–35 yrs.)	Men (22–35 yrs.)
Protein	27%	23%
Iron	26%	46%
Thiamin	13%	9%
Riboflavin	7%	6%

A cup of dry split peas (cooked) provides about 290 calories and the following percentages of the minimum daily recommended allowances for adults:

Nutrient	Women (22–35 yrs.)	Men (22–35 yrs.)
Protein	36%	31%
Iron	23%	42%
Thiamin	37%	26%
Riboflavin	15%	13%

BUYING TIPS

Although there are many varieties of dry beans, peas, and lentils available in the stores, the following buying tips apply for all of them:

● Federal-State Grades—Nearly all peas and lentils and about one-third of all beans are officially inspected before or after processing. However, retail packages of beans, peas, or lentils seldom carry the Federal or State grade.

Developed by the U.S. Department of Agriculture's Agricultural Marketing Service, Federal grades for beans, peas, and lentils are generally based on the following factors: shape, size, color, damage, and foreign material. The more uniform the color and size of the product, the higher the Federal grade will be. Beans, peas, and lentils in the lower grades usually contain more foreign matter and more kernels of uneven size and off-color. Lower qualities are not usually sold through retail stores.

The Federal grades for beans, peas, and lentils you may see on the grocery shelf are normally the highest grades. Some of these higher grades are:

U.S. No. 1—for dry whole or split peas, lentils, and black-eye peas (beans).

U.S. No. 1 Choice Handpicked, or Handpicked—for Great Northern, pinto, and pea beans.

U.S. Extra No. 1 for lima beans, large or small.

Instead of the Federal grade on beans, you might find a State grade which is based on quality factors similar to those for Federal grades.

● Quality factors—If you do not find packages of beans, peas, or lentils marked with Federal or State grades, you can be your own "grader" in a way by looking for the same factors a Federal grader considers.

First, try to buy your beans, peas, or lentils in cellophane bags or other "see through" types of packages, such as cardboard boxes with a cello-phane "window." Then, consider these factors:

Brightness of color—Beans, peas, and lentils should have a bright uniform color. Loss of color usually indicates long storage, lack of freshness, and a product that will take longer to cook. Eating quality, however, is not affected.

Uniformity of size—Look for beans, peas, or lentils of uniform size. Mixed sizes will result in uneven cooking, since smaller beans cook faster than larger ones.

Visible defects—Cracked seed coats, foreign material, and pinholes caused by insect damage are signs of a low quality product.

● Read the label—In addition to the Federal or State grade, the package label can provide other important buying information. By law, the label must contain at least the following basic informa-tion: the name and address of the manufacturer, packer, or distributor, the common or usual name of the product (pea beans, Great Northern beans, etc.), and the weight (given in pounds and ounces).

Other information on the label might include a picture of a suggested way to serve beans, peas, or lentils, and instructions on how to prepare and serve them, including recipes.

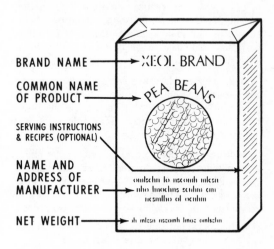

In summary, look for beans, peas, and lentils in cellophane or other clear packages which carry a Federal or State grade. If you can't find graded packages, look for a product with a bright color, beans of uniform size, and no visible damage. Read the label carefully—it may give you important in-structions for preparing the product.

STORAGE TIPS

Dry beans, peas, and lentils should be kept in tightly covered containers and stored in a dry, cool place (50 to 70 degrees Fahrenheit). Stored in this manner, they will keep their quality for several months.

After opening a package, don't mix the contents with that of other packages bought at separate times, particularly several months apart. Mixing packages will result in uneven cooking since older beans take longer to cook than fresher ones. Keep the product in the original package until opened. Then store it in a glass or metal jar or a container with a tight-fitting lid.

PREPARATION TIPS

● Wash beans, peas, and lentils first.

● Dry beans and **whole** peas should be soaked before cooking to reduce the time required for cooking. **Split** peas used in soup and lentils may be boiled **without soaking.** Split peas used for other purposes hold their shape better if soaked for a short time.

● A quick and effective way to soak beans and whole peas is to start by boiling them in water for two minutes. Remove from heat, soak one hour, and they are ready to cook. Soak split peas only ½ hour before cooking them.

● If beans or peas are to be soaked overnight, it is still advantageous to start with the two minute boil because this will mean fewer hard skins. If the beans or peas are to be soaked overnight in a warm room, the brief boil will keep them from souring.

● A teaspoon of salt for each cup of dry beans, peas, or lentils will suit the average taste. For special flavor, add onions, herbs, or meat. Add salt and flavoring only after soaking since salt toughens the surface of the beans and increases cooking time.

● Boil gently and stir very little in order to prevent breaking of skins.

● If preferred, some dry beans and peas—including Great Northern, kidney, large lima, black, cranberry, pea (navy), and pinto beans and whole peas—can be pressure cooked in from 3–10 minutes, depending on variety. Fill pressure cooker no more than one-third full of food and water to allow for expansion. Beans and peas which normally cook in short periods of time should not be pressure-cooked. These include black-eye peas (beans), lentils, and split peas.

● Always remember to allow for expansion of beans, peas, and lentils when cooking. For example, depending on the kind, one cup of the dried beans yields 2 to 2¾ cups of cooked beans.

The following specific information about beans, peas, and lentils should help you decide which product to buy.

BEANS

Beans are among the oldest of foods and today are considered an important staple for millions of people.

They once were considered to be worth their weight in gold—the jeweler's "carat" owes its origin to a pea-like bean on the east coast of Africa.

Beans also once figured very prominently in politics. During the age of the Romans, balloting was done with beans. White beans represented a vote of approval and the dark beans meant a negative vote. Today, beans still play an active role in politics—bean soup is a daily "must" in both the Senate and the House dining rooms in the Nation's Capitol.

Beans undergo rather extensive processing before reaching the consumer. They are delivered to huge processing plants where they are cleaned to remove pods, stems, and other debris. Special machines separate debris by weight (gravity), and then screen the beans by size. Discolored beans are removed by machines equipped with photosensitive electric eyes.

Many varieties of beans may be found on the grocery shelf. Although you will not find all of them, here are some of the more popular varieties, and their uses:

● **Black beans** (or black turtle soup beans)— They are used in thick soups and in Oriental and Mediterranean dishes.

● **Black-eye peas** (also called black-eye beans or "cow peas")—These beans are small, oval-shaped, and creamish white with a black spot on one side. They are used primarily as a main dish vegetable. Black-eye peas **are** beans. There is no difference in the product, but different names are used in some regions of the country.

● **Garbanzo beans**—Known as "chick-peas," these beans are nut-flavored and commonly pickled in vinegar and oil for salads. They can also be used as a main dish vegetable, in the "unpickled" form. Similar beans are cranberry and yellow-eye beans.

● **Great Northern beans**—Larger than but similar to pea beans, these beans are used in soups, salads, casserole dishes, and home baked beans.

● **Kidney beans**—These beans are large and have a red color and kidney shape. They are popular for chili con carne and add zest to salads and many Mexican dishes.

● **Lima beans**—Not widely known as dry beans, lima beans make an excellent main dish vegetable and can be used in casseroles. They are broad and flat. Lima beans come in different sizes, but the size does not affect the quality.

● **Navy beans**—This is a broad term which includes Great Northern, pea, flat small white, and small white beans.

● **Pea beans**—Small, oval, and white, pea beans are a favorite for home baked beans, soups, and casseroles. They hold their shape even when cooked tender.

● **Pinto beans**—These beans are of the same species as the kidney and red beans. Beige-colored and speckled, they are used mainly in salads and chili.

● **Red and pink beans**—Pink beans have a more delicate flavor than red beans. Both are used in many Mexican dishes and chili. They are related to the kidney bean.

PEAS

Dry peas are an interesting and versatile food group that add variety to meals. Dry peas may be green or yellow and may be bought either split or whole.

● **Green dry peas**—This type of dry pea has a more distinct flavor than yellow dry peas. Green dry peas enjoy their greatest popularity in the United States, England, and North European countries and are gaining in popularity in Japan.

● **Yellow dry peas**—This type of dry pea has a less pronounced flavor than other types of peas but is in popular demand in the Southern and Eastern parts of the country. They are also preferred in Eastern Canada, the Caribbean, and South America.

● **Dry split peas**—These peas have had their skins removed and they are mainly used for split pea soup. Dry split peas also combine well with many different foods. How do split peas get split?

Specially grown whole peas are dried and their skins are removed by a special machine. A second machine then breaks the peas in half.

● **Dry whole peas**—These peas are used in making soups, casseroles, puddings, vegetable side dishes, dips, and hors d'oeuvres.

Green and yellow whole peas and green and yellow split peas, although they vary in taste a little, are used interchangeably in many recipes and in making soups. Individual preference is the deciding factor here. Remember, though, there is a difference in soaking procedure for whole and split peas.

Dry peas are served in many ways—"just plain boiled" and served with butter, for example, they serve as a welcome dish with meats, fish, poultry, and game. They can also be served as a puree and they can be made into dips, patties, croquettes, stuffed peppers, and even souffles.

LENTILS

The lentil is an old world legume, that is disc-shaped, about the size of a pea. Thousands of years old, lentils were perhaps the first of the convenience foods. With no coddling at all, they cook to puffed tenderness in a mere half hour. With such a short cooking time, the use of a pressure cooker is not advised. If the cooked lentils are to be drained, as in making salad, save the cooking liquid (which is loaded with nutrients) for a cup of luncheon soup or to use in gravies and stews.

Lentils are an excellent partner with many foods—fruits, vegetables, and meat. To cook, place 2 cups of lentils in a heavy saucepan, and add 5 cups of cold or warm water and 2 teaspoons salt. Bring to boiling point, reduce heat, cover tightly, and boil gently for 30 minutes.

How to Buy FRESH VEGETABLES

Fresh vegetables not only are packed with good-for-you ingredients like vitamins and minerals, but they also add color and variety to your meals.

Properly cooked vegetables add interest and enjoyment as well as nutrition to a meal. Cooking only long enough to make the vegetable tender tends to preserve more flavor and better texture than prolonged cooking.

Thanks to the increased efficiency of marketing and the great strides made in recent years in the produce industry, most of the fresh vegetables on today's market are of good quality. Advanced technology of production methods, mechanical precooling, better shipping and storage methods, and refrigerated displays make possible an abundance of vegetables.

In food stores, many fresh vegetables come washed, trimmed, and prepackaged individually for the convenience of consumers.

GRADES

The Agricultural Marketing Service of the U.S. Department of Agriculture has established grade standards for most fresh vegetables. These standards generally provide two or more grades which describe the quality of vegetables in a lot. The top grade in most cases is either U.S. No. 1 or U.S. Fancy. The standards are used extensively as a basis for trading between growers, shippers, wholesalers and retailers. They are used to a limited extent in sales from retailers to consumers.

The quality of most fresh vegetables can be judged reasonably well by their external appearance. Therefore, except for those products sold in closed consumer-size packages, consumers can make a good selection of fresh vegetables from retail display counters even though they may not bear any grade mark or other identification of quality at this stage of sale.

Use of USDA standards for grades is not required by Federal law. However, some Federal marketing programs set minimum quality levels based on U.S. grades and require official inspection. In addition, a few States require that some products packed for marketing be graded and labeled on the basis of either Federal or State grade standards.

In retail stores, grade designations are often found on packages of potatoes, onions, carrots, and occasionally on other vegetables. Such terms in themselves give little assurance of the quality of the contents of the package. However, if the package also bears the official USDA grade shield or the statement, "Packed under Continuous Inspection of the U.S. Department of Agriculture," or "USDA Inspected," the shopper can buy with a much greater degree of confidence. She has assurance that the product was officially inspected during the packing operation and that, at the time of packing, it met the requirements of the grade shown on the package.

FOOD BUYING TIPS

Demand freshness! Check the characteristic signs of freshness such as bright, lively color and crispness. Vegetables are usually at their best quality and price at the peak of the season.

Handle with care. Use thoughtful care to prevent injury to vegetables. Some vegetables are more hardy than others, but bruising and damage can be prevented by just being careful. The consumer pays for carelessness in the long run.

Shop the plentifuls. The U.S. Department of Agriculture notifies consumers through newspapers and other media when vegetables are in abundant supply across the country.

Don't buy just because of low price. It doesn't pay to buy more vegetables than you can properly store in your refrigerator, or than you can use without waste. Most fresh vegetables can be stored for two to five days, except for root vegetables which can be stored from one to several weeks.

Avoid decay. It's "penny foolish" to buy fresh vegetables affected by decay. Even if you do trim off the decayed area, rapid deterioration is likely to spread to the salvaged area. A few cents extra for vegetables in good condtion is a good investment.

A CONSUMER'S GUIDE TO BUYING FRESH VEGETABLES

There are no set rules in buying vegetables because they all have individual characteristics and values. Experience in personal selection is the best teacher. The following alphabetical list is designed as a handy reference to help you make your selection.

ARTICHOKES

The globe artichoke is the large, unopened flower bud of a plant belonging to the thistle family. The many leaf-like parts making up the bud are called "scales." Produced only in Califorina, artichokes are shipped in limited amounts most of the year, but the peak of the crop comes in April and May.

Look for: Plump, globular artichokes that are heavy in relation to size, and compact with thick, green, fresh-looking scales. Size is not important in relation to quality.

Avoid: Artichokes with large areas of brown on the scales and with spreading scales (a sign of age, indicating drying and toughening of the edible portions), grayish-black discoloration (caused by bruises), mold growth on the scales, and worm injury.

ASPARAGUS

California, New Jersey, Washington, and Michigan are the chief sources of asparagus, available from mid-February through June, with peak supplies from April to June. Very little is available after the end of June.

Look for: Closed, compact tips, smooth, round spears and a fresh appearance. A rich green color should cover most of the spear. Stalks should be tender almost as far down as the green extends.

Avoid: Tips that are open and spread out, moldy or decayed tips, or ribbed spears (spears with up-and-down ridges, or that are not approximately round). These are all signs of aging, and mean tough asparagus and poor flavor. Also avoid excessively sandy asparagus, because sand grains can lodge beneath the scales or in the tips of the spears and are difficult to remove in washing.

BEANS
(Snap Beans)

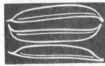

Snap beans, produced commercially in many States, are available throughout the year. Most beans found in the food store will be the common green podded varieties, but large green pole beans and yellow wax beans are occasionally available.

Look for: A fresh, bright appearance with good color for the variety. Get young, tender beans with pods in a firm, crisp condition.

Avoid: Wilted or flabby bean pods, serious blemishes, and decay. Thick, tough, fibrous pods indicate overmaturity.

BEETS

Beets, available year-round, are grown in most parts of the nation, but major growing areas are California, Texas, New Jersey, Ohio, New York, and Colorado. Many beets are sold in bunches with the tops still attached, while others are sold on the basis of weight with the tops removed.

Look for: Beets that are firm, round, with a slender tap root (the large main root), a rich, deep red color, and smooth over most of the surface. If beets are bunched, you can judge their freshness fairly accurately by the condition of the tops. Badly wilted or decayed tops indicate a lack of freshness, but the roots may be satisfactory if they are firm.

Avoid: Elongated beets with round, scaly areas around the top surface—these will be tough, fibrous, and strong-flavored. Also avoid wilted, flabby beets—which have been exposed to the air too long.

BROCCOLI

A member of the cabbage family, and a close relative of cauliflower, broccoli is available throughout the year but—because broccoli grows better in cool weather—is least abundant in July and August.

California is the heaviest producer, but Texas, New Jersey, Oregon, Florida, Pennsylvania, and other States produce large amounts of broccoli.

Look for: A firm, compact cluster of small flower buds, with none opened enough to show the bright yellow flower. Bud clusters should be dark green or sage green—or even green with a decidedly purplish cast. Stems should not be too thick or tough.

Avoid: Broccoli with spread bud clusters, enlarged or open buds, yellowish green color, or wilted condition—signs of overmaturity and overlong display. Also avoid broccoli with soft, slippery, watersoaked spots on the bud cluster. These are signs of decay.

BRUSSELS SPROUTS

Another close relative of the cabbage, Brussels sprouts develop as enlarged buds on a tall stem, one sprout appearing where each main leaf is attached. The "sprouts"

are cut off, and in most cases are packed in small containers. Most Brussels sprouts are produced in California, New York, and Oregon, and some are imported. Although they are often available about 10 months of the year, peak supplies are from October through December.

Look for: A fresh, bright-green color, tight fitting outer leaves, firm body, and freedom from blemishes.

Avoid: Brussels sprouts with yellow or yellowish-green leaves, or leaves which are loose, soft, or wilted. Small holes or ragged leaves may indicate worm injury.

CABBAGE

Three major groups of cabbage varieties are available: smooth-leaved green cabbage, crinkly-leaved green Savoy cabbage, and red cabbage. All types are suitable for any use, although the Savoy and red varieties are more in demand for use in slaws and salads.

Cabbage may be sold fresh (called "new" cabbage) or from storage (called "old" cabbage). New cabbage is available throughout the year, since it is grown in many States. In winter, California, Florida, and Texas market most new cabbage. Many northern States grow cabbage for late summer and fall shipment or to be held in storage for winter sale.

Look for: Firm or hard heads of cabbage that are heavy for their size. Outer leaves should be a good green or red color (depending on type), reasonably fresh, and free from serious blemishes. The outer leaves (called "wrapper" leaves) fit loosely on the head and are usually discarded, but too many loose wrapper leaves on a head cause extra waste.

Some early-crop cabbage may be soft or only fairly firm—but is suitable for immediate use if the leaves are fresh and crisp. Cabbage out of storage is usually trimmed of all outer leaves and lacks green color, but is satisfactory if not wilted or discolored.

Avoid: New cabbage with wilted or decayed outer leaves or with leaves turning decidedly yellow. Worm-eaten outer leaves often indicate that the worm injury penetrates into the head.

Storage cabbage with outer leaves badly discolored, dried, or decayed probably is over-aged. Separation of the stems of leaves from the central stem at the base of the head also indicates over-age.

CARROTS

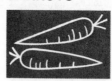

Freshly harvested carrots are available the year round. Most of them are marketed when relatively young, tender, well-colored, and mild-flavored—an ideal stage for use as raw carrot sticks. Larger carrots are packed separately and are used primarily for cooking or shredding. California and Texas market most carrots, but many other States produce large quantities.

Look for: Carrots which are well formed, smooth, well-colored, and firm.

Avoid: Roots with large green "sunburned" areas at the top (which must be trimmed) and roots which are flabby from wilting or show spots of soft decay.

CAULIFLOWER

Though most abundant from September through January, cauliflower is available during every month of the year. California, New York, Oregon, Texas, and Michigan are major sources. The white, edible portion is called the curd and the heavy outer leaf covering, the jacket leaves. Cauliflower is generally sold with most of the jacket leaves removed, and is wrapped in clear plastic film.

Look for: White to creamy-white, compact, solid and clean curds. A slightly granular or "ricey" texture of the curd will not hurt the eating quality if the surface is compact. Ignore small green leaflets extending through the curd. If jacket leaves are attached, a good green color is a sign of freshness.

Avoid: A spreading of the curd—a sign of aging or overmaturity. Also avoid severe wilting or many discolored spots, on the curd. A smudgy or speckled appearance of the curd is a sign of insect injury, mold growth or decay and should be avoided.

CELERY

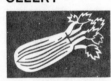

Celery, a popular vegetable for a variety of uses, is available throughout the year. Production is concentrated in California, Florida, Michigan, and New York. Most celery is of the so-called "Pascal" type which includes thick-branched, green varieties.

Look for: Freshness and crispness in celery. The stalk should have a solid, rigid feel and leaflets should be fresh or only slightly wilted. Also look for a glossy surface, stalks of light green or medium green, and mostly green leaflets.

Avoid: Wilted celery and celery with flabby upper branches or leaf stems. You can freshen celery somewhat by placing the butt end in water, but badly wilted celery will never become really fresh again.

Also avoid celery with pithy, hollow, or discolored centers in the branches. Celery with internal discoloration will show some gray or brown on the inside surface of the larger branches near where they are attached to the base of the stalk.

Avoid celery with: 1. "Blackheart," a brown or black discoloration of the small center branches; 2. Insect injury in the center branches or the insides of outer branches; 3. Long, thick seed-stem in place of the usually small, tender heart branches.

CHARD (See Greens)

CHINESE CABBAGE

Primarily a salad vegetable, Chinese cabbage plants are elongated, with some varieties developing a firm head and others an open, leafy form.

Look for: Fresh, crisp, green plants that are free from blemishes or decay.

Avoid: Wilted or yellowed plants.

CHICORY, ENDIVE, ESCAROLE

These vegetables, used mainly in salads, are available practically all year round—but primarily in the winter and spring. Chicory or endive has narrow, notched edges, and crinkly leaves resembling the dandelion leaf. Chicory plants often have "blanched" yellowish leaves in the center which are preferred by many persons. Escarole leaves are much broader and less crinkly than those of chicory.

Look for: Freshness, crispness, tenderness, and a good green color of the outer leaves.

Avoid: Plants with leaves which have brownish or yellowish discoloration or which have insect injury.

Note: Witloof or Belgian endive is a compact, cigar-shaped plant which is creamy white from blanching. The small shoots are kept from becoming green by being grown in complete darkness.

COLLARDS (See Greens)

CORN

Sweet corn is available practically every month of the year, but is most plentiful from early May until mid - September. Most supplies are yellow-kernal corn, but some white corn is sold. Sweet corn is produced in a large number of States during the spring and summer, but most mid-winter supplies come from south Florida.

For best quality, corn should be refrigerated immediately after being picked. Corn will retain fairly good quality for a number of days, if it has been kept cold and moist since harvesting. For the same reason, it should be placed in the home refrigerator as soon as possible and kept moist until used.

Look for: Fresh, succulent husks with good green color, silk-ends that are free from decay or worm injury, and stem ends (opposite from the silk) that are not too discolored or dried.

Select ears that are well covered with plump, not-too-mature kernels.

Avoid: Ears with under-developed kernels which lack yellow color (in yellow corn), old ears with very large kernels, and ears with dark yellow kernels with depressed areas on the outer surface.

Also avoid ears of corn with yellowed, wilted, or dried husks, or discolored and dried-out stem ends.

CUCUMBERS

Although cucumbers are produced at various times in many States— and imported during the colder months — the supply is most plentiful in the summer months.

Look for: Cucumbers with good green color which are firm over their entire length. They should be well-shaped and well-developed, but should not be too large in diameter. Good cucumbers typically have many small lumps on their surfaces. They may also have some white or greenish-white color and still be of top quality.

Avoid: Overgrown cucumbers which are large in diameter and have a dull color, turning yellowish. Also avoid cucumbers with withered or shriveled ends—signs of toughness and bitter flavor.

EGGPLANT

Eggplant is most plentiful during the late summer, but is available all year to some extent.

Look for: Firm, heavy, smooth, and uniformly dark purple egg plants.

Avoid: Those which are poorly colored, soft, shriveled, cut, or which show decay in the form of irregular dark-brown spots.

ENDIVE, ESCAROLE (See Chicory)

GREENS

A large number of widely differing species of plants are grown for uses as "greens." The better known kinds are spinach, kale, collards, turnips, beets, chard, mustard, broccoli leaves, chicory, endive, escarole, dandelion, cress, and sorrel. Many others, some of them wild, are also used to a limited extent as greens.

Look for: Leaves that are fresh, young, tender, free from blemishes, and which have a good, healthy green color. Beet tops and ruby chard show reddish color.

Avoid: Leaves with coarse, fibrous stems, yellowish-green color, softness (a sign of decay), or a wilted condition. Also avoid greens with evidence of insects—especially aphids—which are sometimes hard to see, and equally hard to wash away.

KALE (See Greens)

LETTUCE

Among the Nation's leading vegetables, lettuce owes its prominence to the growing popularity of salads in our diet. It's available throughout the year, at various seasons, from California, Arizona, New York, New Jersey, Texas, Colorado, New Mexico, Wisconsin, and other States. Four types of lettuce are generally sold: iceburg, butter-head, Romaine, and leaf.

Iceberg lettuce is the major group. Heads are large, round, and solid, with medium-green outer leaves and lighter green or pale-green inner leaves.

Butter-head lettuce, including the Big Boston and Bibb varieties, has a smaller head than Iceberg. This type will be slightly flat on top and have soft, succulent, light-green leaves in a rosette pattern in the center.

Romaine lettuce plants are tall and cylindrical with crisp, dark-green leaves in a loosely folded head.

Leaf Lettuce includes many varieties—none with a compact head. Leaves are broad, tender, succulent, fairly smooth and vary in color according to variety. It is grown mainly in greenhouses or on truck farms and sold locally.

Look for: Signs of freshness in lettuce. For Iceberg lettuce and Romaine, the leaves should be crisp. Other lettuce types will have a softer texture, but leaves should not be wilted. Look for a good, bright color—in most varieties, medium to light green.

Avoid: Heads of iceberg type which are very hard and which lack green color (signs of over-maturity). Such heads sometimes develop discoloration in the center of the leaves (the "mid-ribs"), and may have a less attractive flavor. Also avoid heads with irregular shapes and hard bumps on top, which indicates the presence of overgrown central stems.

Check the lettuce for tipburn, a tan or brown area (dead tissue) around the margins of the leaves. Look for tipburn on the edges of the head leaves. Slight discoloration of the outer or wrapper leaves will usually not hurt the quality of the lettuce, but serious discoloration or soft decay definitely should be avoided.

MELONS

Selection of melons is discussed in "How to Buy Fresh Fruits," on page 57.

MUSHROOMS

Grown in houses, cellars, or caves, mushrooms are available the year round in varying amounts. Most come from Pennsylvania, but many are produced in California, New York, Ohio, and Illinois and other States.

We usually describe mushrooms as having caps —the wide portion on top, gills—the numerous rows of paper-thin tissue seen underneath the cap when it opens, and a stem.

Look for: Young mushrooms that are small to medium in size. Caps should be either closed around the stem or moderately open with pink or light-tan gills. The surface of the cap should be white or creamy—or light brown from some producing areas.

Avoid: Overripe mushrooms (shown by wide-open caps and dark, discolored gills underneath) and those with pitted or seriously discolored caps.

OKRA

Okra is the immature seed pod of the okra plant, grown and marketed locally in the southern states.

Look for: Tender pods (the tips will bend with very slight pressure) under 4-½ inches long. They should have a bright green color and be free from blemishes.

Avoid: Tough, fibrous pods, indicated by tips which are stiff and resist bending, or by a very hard body of the pod, or by pale, faded green color.

ONIONS

The many varieties of onions grown commercially fall into three general classes:

Globe onions are the most common group, and are considered primarily cooking onions. There are many varieties, mostly with yellow skins, but also some white and red-skinned types. Globe onions are predominantly round to oval, and have rather pungent flavor. They are available in quantity during the late summer, fall, and winter. Most fall in the medium size range, but in some cases the smaller onions are packed and sold separately.

Granex-Grano onions are available during the spring and summer, coming from the warmer growing areas. Most are yellow-skinned; a few are white. The shape tends to be less round and less symmetrical than the globes, ranging from somewhat flattened to top shaped. Rather mild in flavor, they are considered ideal for slicing and eating raw and good for cooking. In size they range from medium to large.

Spanish onions resemble globe onions in shape, but they are generally much larger. Most varieties are yellow, but some are white-skinned. They are mild in flavor, often called "sweet Spanish," and are ideal for slicing or for salads. Sometimes the medium sizes are packed separately from the large ones (3 inches or more in diameter). Spanish type onions are generally available in moderate supply during fall and winter.

Major onion growing areas are California, New York, Texas, Michigan, Colorado, Oregon, and Idaho.

Look for: Hard or firm onions which are dry and have small necks. They should be covered with papery outer scales and reasonably free from green sunburn spots, and other blemishes.

Avoid: Onions with wet or very soft necks, which usually are immature or affected by decay. Also avoid onions with thick, hollow, woody centers in the neck or with fresh sprouts.

ONIONS, (GREEN), SHALLOTS, LEEKS

All three of these (sometimes called scallions) are similiar in appearance, but are somewhat different in nature.

Green onions are ordinary onions harvested very young. They have very little or no bulb formation, and their tops are tubular.

Shallots are similar to green onions, but grow in clusters and have practically no swelling at the base.

Leeks are larger than shallots, and have slight bulb formation and broad, flat, dark-green tops.

Sold in small, tied bunches, they are all available to some extent throughout the entire year, but are most plentiful in the spring and summer.

Look for: Bunches with fresh, crisp, green tops. They should have well-blanched (white) portions extending two or three inches up from the root end.

Avoid: Yellowing, wilted, discolored, or decayed tops (indicating flabby, tough, or fibrous condition of the edible portions). Bruised tops will not affect the eating quality of the bulbs, if the tops are removed.

PARSLEY

Parsley, which ranks at the top among vegetables in vitamin A content, can be a valuable addition to your diet as well as a taste treat if you consider it as a food instead of just a decorative garnish. It is generally available the year round.

Look for: Fresh, crisp, bright-green leaves, for both the curled-leaf and the flat-leaf types of parsley. Slightly wilted leaves can be freshened by trimming off the ends of the stems and placing them in cold water.

PARSNIPS

Although available to some extent throughout the year, parsnips are primarily a late winter vegetable. This is because the flavor becomes sweeter and more desirable after long exposure to cold temperatures (below 40° F).

Look for: Parsnips of small or medium width that are well formed, smooth, firm, and free from serious blemishes or decay.

Avoid: Large, coarse roots (which probably have woody, fibrous, or pithy centers), and badly wilted and flabby roots (which will be tough when cooked).

PEPPERS

Most of the peppers you'll find are the sweet green peppers, available in varying amounts throughout the year, but most plentiful during the late summer. (Fully matured peppers of the same type have a bright red color.)

Look for: Medium to dark green color, glossy sheen, relatively heavy weight, and firm walls or sides.

Avoid: Peppers with very thin walls (shown by light weight and flimsy sides), peppers that are wilted or flabby with cuts or punctures through the walls, and peppers with soft watery spots on the sides (evidence of decay).

POTATOES

For practical purposes, potatoes can be put into three groups, although the distinctions between them are not clear-cut, and there is much overlapping.

"New" potatoes is a term most frequently used to describe those freshly harvested and marketed during the late winter or early spring. The name is also widely used in later crop producing areas to designate freshly dug potatoes which are not quite fully matured. Best use of new potatoes is boiling or creaming. They vary widely in size and shape, depending upon variety, but are likely to be affected by "skinning" or "feathering" of the outer layer of skin. This skinning usually affects only their appearance.

General purpose potatoes include the great majority of supplies offered for sale in the markets, both round and long types. With the aid of air-cooled storages, they are amply available throughout the year. As the term implies, they are used for boiling, frying and baking, although many of the common varieties are not considered to be best for baking.

Baking Potatoes. Both the variety and the area where grown are important factors affecting baking quality. The Russet Burbank, a long variety with fine, scaly netting on the skin is the most widely grown and best known among this group.

Look for: (in new potatoes) Well-shaped, firm potatoes that are free from blemishes and sunburn (a green discoloration under the skin). Some amount of skinned surface is normal, but potatoes with large skinned and discolored areas are undesirable.

Look for: (in general purpose and baking potatoes) Reasonably smooth, well-shaped, firm potatoes free from blemishes, sunburn, and decay. These potatoes should be relatively free from skinned surfaces.

Avoid: Potatoes with large cuts or bruises (they'll mean waste in peeling), those with a green color (probably caused by sunburn or exposure to light in the store), and potatoes showing any signs of decay.

Also avoid sprouted or shriveled potatoes.

RADISHES

Radishes, available the year round, are most plentiful from May through July. California and Florida produce most of our winter and spring supplies, while several Northern States provide radishes the rest of the year.

Look for: Medium size radishes (¾ to 1-⅛ inches in diameter) that are plump, round, firm, and of a good red color.

Avoid: Very large or flabby radishes (likely to have pithy centers). Also avoid radishes with yellow or decayed tops (sign of over-age).

RHUBARB

This highly specialized vegetable is used like a fruit in sweetened sauces and pies. Very limited supplies are available during most of the year, with most supplies available from January to June.

Look for: Fresh, firm rhubarb stems with a bright, glossy appearance. Stems should have a large amount of pink or red color, although many good-quality stems will be predominantly light green. Be sure the stem is tender and not fibrous.

Avoid: Either very slender or extremely thick stems, which are likely to be tough and stringy. Also avoid rhubarb that is wilted and flabby.

RUTABAGAS (See Turnips)

SPINACH (See Greens)

SQUASH (Summer)

Summer squash includes those varieties which are harvested while still immature and when the entire squash is tender and edible. They include the yellow *Crookneck,* the large yellow *Straightneck,* the greenish-white *Patty Pan,* and the slender green *Zucchini* and *Italian Marrow.* Some of these squash are available at all times of the year.

Look for: Squash that are tender and well developed, firm, fresh-appearing, and well formed. You can identify a tender squash because the skin is glossy instead of dull, and it is neither hard nor tough.

Avoid: Stale or overmature squash, which will have a dull appearance and a hard, tough surface. Such squash usually have enlarged seeds and dry, stringy flesh.

SQUASH (Fall and Winter)

Winter squashes are those varieties which are marketed only when fully mature. Some of the most important varieties are the small corrugated *Acorn* (available all year round), *Butternut, Buttercup,* green and blue *Hubbard,* green and gold *Delicious,* and *Banana.* Winter squash is most plentiful from early fall until late winter.

Look for: Full maturity, indicated by a hard, tough rind. Also look for squash that is heavy for its size (meaning a thick wall, and more edible flesh). Slight variations in skin color do not affect flavor.

Avoid: Squash with cuts, punctures, sunken spots, or moldy spots on the rind—all indications of decay. A tender rind indicates immaturity which is a sign of poor eating quality in winter squash varieties.

SWEETPOTATOES

Two types of sweetpotatoes are available in varying amounts the year round.

Moist sweetpotatoes, sometimes called yams, are the most common type. They have orange colored flesh and are very sweet. The true yam is the root of a tropical vine which is not grown commercially in the U.S.

Dry sweetpotatoes have a pale colored flesh, low in moisture. Their production has dwindled rapidly.

Most sweetpotatoes are grown in the Southern tier and some Eastern States, in an area from Texas to New Jersey. California is also a heavy producer.

Look for: Well-shaped, firm sweet potatoes with smooth, bright, uniformly colored skins, free from signs of decay. Because they are more perishable than Irish potatoes, extra care should be used in selecting sweetpotatoes.

Avoid: Sweetpotatoes with worm holes, cuts, grub injury, or any other defects which penetrate the skin; this causes waste and can readily lead to decay. Even if you cut away the decayed portion, the remainder of the potato flesh which looks normal may have a bad taste.

Decay is the worst problem with sweetpotatoes and is of three types: wet, soft decay, dry firm decay which begins at the end of the potato, making it discolored and shriveled; and dry rot in the form of sunken, discolored areas on the sides of the potato.

Sweetpotatoes should not be stored in the refrigerator.

TOMATOES

Extremely popular and nutritious, tomatoes are in moderate to liberal supply throughout the year. Florida, California, Texas, and a number of other States are major producers, but imports supplement domestic supplies from late winter to early spring.

Best flavor usually comes from "home grown" tomatoes produced on nearby farms. This type of tomato is allowed to ripen completely before being picked. Many areas, however, now ship tomatoes which are picked after the color has begun to change from green to pink. These tomatoes have flavor almost as satisfying as the home-grown ones.

If your tomatoes need further ripening, keep them in a warm place. Unless they are fully ripened, do not store tomatoes in a refrigerator— the cold temperatures might keep them from ripening later on. Once tomatoes are ripe, however, you may keep them in the refrigerator for some time.

Look for: Tomatoes which are well formed, smooth, well ripened, and reasonably free from blemishes.

For fully ripe fruit, look for an overall rich red color and a slight softness. Softness is easily detected by gentle handling.

For tomatoes slightly less than fully ripe, look for firm texture and color ranging from pink to light red.

Avoid: Overripe and bruised tomatoes (they're both soft and watery) and tomatoes with sunburn (green or yellow areas near the stem scar) and growth cracks (deep cracks around the stem scar). Also avoid decayed tomatoes which will have soft, water-soaked spots, depressed areas, or surface mold.

TURNIPS

The most popular *turnip* has white flesh and a purple top (reddish-purple tinting of upper surface). It may be sold "topped" (with leaves removed) or in bunches with tops still on, and is available in some food stores most of the year.

Rutabagas are distinctly yellow-fleshed, large-sized relatives of turnips. They are available generally in the fall and winter, but cold-storage rutabagas are often available in the spring. Late winter storage rutabagas are sometimes coated

with a thin layer of paraffin in order to prevent loss of moisture and shriveling. The paraffin is readily removed with the peeling before cooking.

Look for: (in turnips) Small or medium size, smooth, fairly round, and firm vegetables. If sold in bunches, the tops should be fresh and should have a good green color.

Avoid: Large turnips with too many leaf scars around the top and with obvious fibrous roots.

Look for: (in rutabagas) Heavy weight for their size, generally smooth, round or moderately elongated shape, and firmness.

Avoid: Rutabagas with skin punctures, deep cuts or decay.

WATERCRESS

Watercress is a small, round-leaved plant that grows naturally (or may be cultivated) along the banks of freshwater streams and ponds. It is prized as an ingredient of mixed green salads and as a garnish, because of its spicy flavor. Also its very high vitamin A content makes it a valuable addition to the diet. Watercress is available in limited supply through most of the year.

Look for: Watercress that is fresh, crisp, and rich green.

Avoid: Bunches with yellow, wilted, or decayed leaves.

How to Buy POTATOES

By Laurence E. Ide, Head
Fresh Products Standardization
Fruit and Vegetable Division
Agricultural Marketing Service

INTRODUCTION

Boiled, baked or fried; hot or cold; plain or fancy—potatoes are one of our most popular vegetables. In fact, each American eats about 60 pounds of fresh potatoes each year.

To help assure quality in the potatoes you buy, the U.S. Department of Agriculture has established grade standards for potatoes. U.S. No. 1 is the grade or quality level you will find in most retail stores.

USDA provides a voluntary grading service to growers, shippers, wholesalers, and others, for a fee. About 65 percent of the potatoes that are marketed fresh are officially graded in producing areas (at the packing plant from which they are shipped to market) by USDA's Agricultural Marketing Service in cooperation with State agencies.

The U.S. grades are a good guide to quality and were revised to give you better potatoes than before. This booklet describes the revised standards and gives other useful tips on buying, handling, and storing potatoes. It also explains how potatoes are handled from digging to packing.

POTATO GROWING AND MARKETING

Potatoes are produced in every State, but about half of the commercial crop is grown in Idaho, Maine, California, and Washington.

Most of our year-round supply of fresh potatoes is harvested in September or October. These fall crop potatoes are stored for 1 to 9 months before shipment to retail outlets.

Many potatoes, however, are freshly harvested and marketed from January through September. These are called "new" potatoes. This term is also used to describe freshly-dug fall crop potatoes which are not quite fully matured.

Most harvesting is done by potato combines which dig the potatoes out of the ground and move them up a conveyor that shakes them, allows soil to drop through, and conveys the potatoes directly into containers or trucks. Usually several workers on the combine pick out any vines, stones, or other debris. A few harvesters also have built-in devices for removing debris.

Potatoes are usually brushed or washed at the packinghouse. Dirty potatoes are unattractive, and the dirt itself contributes weight for which the buyer is paying.

After cleaning, potatoes are mechanically sized and are then sorted into grades by packinghouse workers. The potatoes are packed according to grade and size. The grade is often certified during packing by Federal-State inspectors.

Over 40 percent of the fresh potatoes are now marketed at retail stores in consumer unit packages—generally 5, 10, 15, or 20 pound bags.

Common types of bags are film (mostly polyethylene), open mesh, paper with mesh or film window, or plain paper. The trend is toward packing so the shopper can see the contents.

Potatoes may be packaged in consumer units at the packinghouse (at shipping point) or at wholesale houses in city terminal markets. Retail chains also do a good deal of packing in consumer units in their central warehouses.

Packing is largely mechanized, and bags are generally check-weighed afterwards to ensure that they are slightly overweight and thus allow for shrinkage in marketing.

Red potatoes and some white varieties are sometimes treated with colored or clear wax before shipment to improve their appearance. The Food and Drug Administration requires that potatoes so treated be plainly marked. Under the Federal Food, Drug, and Cosmetic Act, it is illegal to color "white"-skinned potatoes red or to use colored wax to make potatoes appear fresher or of better quality. Several producing States have banned all use of artificial color.

U. S. GRADE

NO. 1

U.S. GRADES

The first U.S. quality standards for potatoes were developed in 1917 to help potato growers and shippers market their product in wholesale channels. At that time, most potatoes were sold in bulk.

Since then, most potatoes have been marketed under the U.S. No. 1 grade, and bags of potatoes in retail stores are often labeled U.S. No. 1.

The U.S. grade standards have been revised a number of times through the years to keep up with changes in production and marketing practices and in consumer preferences.

In recent years, however, consumers have complained that a bag of U.S. No. 1 potatoes had too wide a range of sizes; that the potatoes weren't clean enough; and that cuts, bruises, and other defects caused too much waste. Some growers, packers, and shippers also believed that the U.S. No. 1 grade covered too wide a range of quality.

So the Agricultural Marketing Service has again revised the grade standards for potatoes.

Effective September 1, 1971, the revised standards are intended to result in cleaner, more uniformly sized potatoes with fewer defects.

To provide for some margin of error in sizing, grading, cleaning, and packing potatoes, the standards permit a small percentage of offsize or undergrade potatoes in all grades. Before setting tolerances for defects, for example, USDA studies how much damage is reasonable because mechanical harvesting and packing practices in themselves cause a certain amount of unavoidable cuts, bruises, and other defects.

The new standards replace the previous top grade, U.S. Fancy, with a new grade, *U.S. Extra No. 1*. U.S. Fancy was seldom used by the potato industry because the requirements were too strict; a very small percentage of the potato crop could meet the grade.

Now, U.S. Extra No. 1 potatoes are the premium grade for consumers who want to buy the

best. The tolerances for defects are stricter than those for U.S. No. 1, and potatoes in this grade can only be slightly affected by internal defects or sprouts. The minimum size is 2¼ inches in diameter or 5 ounces in weight. Variation in size of potatoes within a package is limited. Generally, they must vary by no more than 1¼ inches or 6 ounces.

Under the revised standards, consumers will also find that potatoes marked *U.S. No. 1* are better than before.

The revision reduces the tolerances for defects so that there will be fewer potatoes with cuts, bruises, sprouts, or decay in consumer packages.

In addition, the revision sets up optional size designations which packers may use. If potatoes are labeled with these size designations, they must be within the size ranges shown on the next page.

The consumer might also find U.S. No. 1 potatoes labeled Size A. Such potatoes must be at least 1⅞ inches in diameter, and 40 percent of the potatoes must be 2½ inches in diameter or 6 ounces in weight or larger.

If the size is not designated, the minimum for U.S. No. 1 potatoes is 1⅞ inches in diameter; there is no maximum.

Use of the U.S. grade standards or the Federal-State Inspection Service is voluntary, except where required by State law or certain regulations.

The inspection service, operated jointly by USDA's Agricultural Marketing Service and cooperating State agencies, offers official, impartial, third-party inspection of potatoes, on a fee basis. Shipping point inspection establishes what the quality is at time of shipment, both for sales purposes and for verifying compliance with contract terms. Some packers also find official inspection valuable as a quality-control tool.

Although grade labeling is not required by Federal law, even when potatoes have been officially graded, the U.S. grade is often shown on consumer packages in retail stores. Sometimes, packers label their potatoes by grade whether the potatoes were officially graded or not. But these potatoes should meet the standards if they are so labeled.

Range Under Optimal Sizing

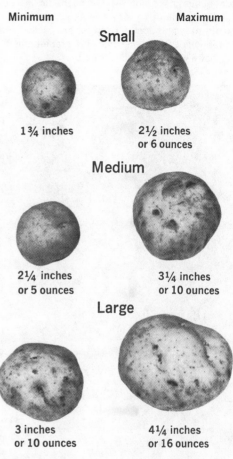

Minimum   Maximum

Small

1¾ inches   2½ inches
                              or 6 ounces

Medium

2¼ inches   3¼ inches
or 5 ounces   or 10 ounces

Large

3 inches   4¼ inches
or 10 ounces   or 16 ounces

Range If Size Is Not Designated

1⅞ inches   (no maximum)
(minimum)

USDA and cooperating State agencies also offer continuous inspection, which means an inspector checks the entire packing operation as well as the quality of the product. If potatoes are packed under continuous USDA inspection, the grade name may be shown within the official shield.

TYPES OF POTATOES

Varieties of potatoes are classified by their shape and skin color. Potatoes are long or round, and their skins may be "white" (the regular white to buff color), red, or russet (normally having a brownish, rough, scaly or netted skin).

The principal varieties are the Russet Burbank (long russet), the White Rose (long white), the Ka-tahdin (round white), and the Red Pontiac (round red). Other varieties are available in different regions at specific times of the year, and some new varieties such as the Norgold Russet (a long to blocky, lightly russeted potato) and the Norland (a round red) are becoming increasingly popular.

As far as the consumer is concerned, potatoes can also be classified by use. There are "new" potatoes, general purpose potatoes, and baking potatoes.

"New" potatoes are best when boiled. They are generally harvested before the skins have "set" and because of immaturity may be "skinned" or "feathered" during handling.

General purpose potatoes, both round and long types, comprise the great majority of supplies. They are available year-round. As the term implies, they are used for boiling, frying, and baking.

Potatoes grown specifically for their baking quality are also available. The most widely grown and best known baking potato is the Russet Burbank.

BUYING TIPS

The revision of the U.S. standards is an attempt to bring the quality of potatoes more into line with what consumers want. So potatoes in bags labeled U.S. No. 1 now should be cleaner and firmer and have fewer defects than in the past.

When shopping for potatoes, look for those that are firm, well shaped, and smooth, with few eyes.

The potatoes should be free from large cuts, growth cracks, bruises, skinned areas, and decay. Some amount of skinning is normal in new potatoes, but avoid new potatoes with large skinned and discolored areas.

Don't buy potatoes that are green. Greening is caused by exposure to natural or artificial light. Sometimes only the skin is affected, but greening may penetrate the flesh. The green portions contain the alkaloid solanin which causes a bitter flavor and is said to be poisonous to some people.

Also avoid badly sprouted or shriveled potatoes. You may find potatoes with second growth. These irregular, knob-shaped growths are considered defects because they are likely to cause quite a bit of waste.

A "smell test" can also help you select potatoes. If the potatoes smell musty or moldy, the flavor may be affected.

It is impossible to detect internal defects without cutting the potato, but if you find that some of the potatoes you have bought are hollow in the center or have severe internal discoloration, take them back to your grocer for replacement.

Consumer unit bags generally carry information about the contents such as the type and origin of the potatoes, the grade, and the weight.

HANDLING AND STORAGE TIPS

Potatoes are nearly as delicate as apples. They can get bruised all the way from the digging machine in the field to your home storage bin. So handle the potatoes you buy with care.

If stored properly, general purpose and baking potatoes will keep for several months; new potatoes will keep for several weeks.

Look potatoes over before you store them. Set aside any that are bruised or cracked and use them first.

Don't wash potatoes before you store them. As it does with most other fresh produce, dampness increases the likelihood of decay.

Store potatoes in a cool (45° to 50° F., if possible), dark place, with good ventilation.

Potatoes stored at 70° to 80° F. should be used within a week. The higher temperature often causes sprouting and shriveling.

Potatoes stored below 40° F. for a week or more may develop a sweet taste because some of the starch changes to sugar. To improve their flavor, store them at a higher temperature for 1 to 2 weeks before using them.

QUESTIONS ABOUT POTATOES

Are potatoes more fattening than other foods? No. A boiled, pressure-cooked, or baked medium-sized potato provides only about 100 calories (approximately the same amount as a large apple or banana) and has no more carbohydrate value than these fruits. It's the fats, gravies, and sauces commonly served with potatoes that increase the calories. Fried potatoes, for example, may be 2 to 4 times as high in calories as a plain baked potato.

What can I do if I can't find bags of medium-sized potatoes at my store? Ask your grocer to get them or pick them from the bulk display.

What causes internal defects? One internal defect, hollow heart (an irregular hole at the center of the potato) is caused by excessively rapid growth.

Another common internal defect is internal discoloration. Internal discoloration may be caused by improper field or storage conditions, freezing, or disease. Each causes a different type of discoloration. Do not use potatoes with severe internal discoloration.

Why is the flesh red in some red-skinned potatoes? These potatoes were probably artificially colored. Some packers believe the coloring makes the potatoes more attractive to consumers.

Under the revised U.S. No. 1 grade, artificial coloring which is unsightly, which conceals any other defects that cause damage, or which causes more than 5 percent waste when removed is considered a defect. If you find that coloring has penetrated the flesh and causes excessive waste, return the potatoes to your grocer.

What should I do if I find a rock in a bag of potatoes? Simply return the rock to your grocer, who will give you the rock's weight in potatoes. Rocks sometimes get into bags of potatoes because most harvesting and packing today is done by machine. Many rocks resemble potatoes in both shape and color.

How to Buy CANNED and FROZEN VEGETABLES

By Edward R. Thompson, Marketing Specialist,
Fruit and Vegetable Division,
Agricultural Marketing Service.

Introduction

Canned and frozen vegetables provide the vitamins, minerals, and food energy we need as part of our daily diets.

These easy-to-prepare foods are not only a convenience, they are a necessity, especially when fresh vegetables are out of season.

All canned and frozen vegetables are wholesome and nutritious, but they can differ in quality —the difference in quality means a difference in taste, texture, and appearance of the vegetable, and its price, too.

If you've been selecting canned or frozen vegetables by habit, or can't tell which can or package would be best for the use you have in mind, here's some information that can help you make a wise choice.

Check the Quality

The Agricultural Marketing Service of the U.S. Department of Agriculture has established grades of quality for many canned and frozen vegetables. The U.S. grade standards are used extensively by processors, buyers, and others in wholesale trading, as a basis for establishing the value of a product. If a vegetable is packed under continuous USDA inspection, the individual cans and packages may carry the U.S. grade name:

U.S. Grade A or Fancy   Grade A vegetables are carefully selected for color, tenderness, and freedom from blemishes. They are the most tender, succulent, and flavorful vegetables produced.

U.S. Grade B or Extra Standard   Grade B vegetables are of excellent quality but not quite so well selected for color and tenderness as Grade A. They are usually slightly more mature and therefore have a slightly different taste than the more succulent vegetables in Grade A.

U.S. Grade C or Standard   Grade C vegetables are not so uniform in color and flavor as vegetables in the higher grades and they are usually more mature. They are a thrifty buy when appearance is not too important — for instance, if you're using the vegetables as an ingredient in soup or souffle.

Packed under continuous inspection of the U.S. Department of Agriculture   This statement may be given along with the grade name or it may be shown by itself. It provides assurance of a wholesome product of at least minimum quality.

The grade names and the statement, "Packed under continuous inspection of the U.S. Department of Agriculture," may also appear within shields.

Use of the U.S. grade standards and inspection service is voluntary, and paid for by the user. But most canned and frozen vegetables are packed and priced according to their quality even though a grade is not shown on the label. Sometimes the grade name is indicated without the "U.S." in front of it—for example, "Fancy" or "Grade A." A canned or frozen vegetable with this designation must measure up to the quality stated, even though it has not been officially inspected for grade.

The brand name of a frozen or canned vegetable may also be an indication of quality. Producers of nationally advertised products spend considerable effort to maintain the same quality year after year. Unadvertised brands may also offer an assurance of quality, often at a slightly lower price. And many stores, particularly chainstores, carry two or more qualities under their own name labels (private labels).

What's on the Label

Fair packaging and labeling regulations should enable you to take a quick look at the label on a can or package of vegetables and see just what you are getting. They should also make it easier for you to compare prices. The regulations require that the following information be given on the label of the can or package as it faces the customer:

● The common or usual name of the product and its form or style. The style—for example, whole, sliced, or diced—may be illustrated rather than printed on the label.

● The net contents in total ounces, as well as pounds and ounces, if the can or package contains 1 pound or more, or less than 4 pounds.

Labels may also give the grade, variety, size, and maturity of the vegetable; seasonings; the number of servings; cooking directions; and recipes or serving ideas. If the number of servings is given, the law requires that the size of the serving must be stated in common measures—ounces or cups—so the buyer will know just how much this serving is.

If the product has been packed under continuous inspection by USDA, the official grade name may also appear on the label, together with the shield indicating that the product has been packed under continuous inspection.

Sizes and Servings

One-half cup is the serving size commonly used for adults for most cooked vegetables. Small children and light eaters are often satisfied with smaller portions—one-fourth or one-third cup.

Deciding which size can or package you should buy is sometimes difficult, because canned and frozen vegetables are packed by net weight rather than volume. Also, the number of cups obtained from a particular size of container varies for different vegetables.

The chart on the next page shows the approximate amount of cooked vegetable obtained from average container sizes of frozen and canned vegetables. This chart should help you tell how many cans or packages you need, or if you should buy smaller or larger sizes.

Vegetable	Cans		Frozen packages	
	Size of container	Cups	Size of container	Cups
Asparagus, cut...	14 oz.	1⅓	10 oz.	1¼
Beans, green or wax, cut.........	15½ oz.	1¾	9 oz.	1⅔
Beans, lima	16 oz.	1¾	10 oz.	1⅔
Beets, sliced, diced or whole	16 oz.	1¾	—	—
Broccoli, cut	—	—	10 oz.	1½
Carrots, diced or sliced........	16 oz.	1¾	10 oz.	1⅔
Cauliflower.........	—	—	10 oz.	1½
Corn, whole kernel..	16 oz.	1⅔	10 oz.	1½
Kale	15 oz.	1⅓	10 oz.	1⅛
Okra................	15½ oz.	1¾	10 oz.	1¼
Peas................	16 oz.	1¾	10 oz.	1⅔
Potatoes, french fried.............	—	—	9 oz.	1⅔
Spinach	15 oz.	1⅓	10 oz.	1¼
Summer squash, sliced...........	—	—	10 oz.	1⅓
Tomatoes..........	16 oz.	1⅞	—	—

Approximate amount of cooked vegetable obtained from:

The most common container sizes for canned vegetables are given below, along with the industry terms used for these sizes. Industry terms for containers of canned vegetables are sometimes given in recipes.

Net weight	Industry term	
8 oz.	8 oz. ———	
10½ to 12 oz.	Picnic ———	
16 to 17 oz.	No. 303 ———	
20 oz. (1 lb. 4 oz.)	No. 2 ———	
29 oz. (1 lb. 13 oz.)	No. 2½ ———	
46 oz. (2 lb. 14 oz.)	No. 3 Special —	

Common package sizes for frozen vegetables are 8, 9, 10, 12, 16, 24, and 32 ounces. Some frozen vegetables are also packaged in large plastic bags. You may find it more economical to buy the large plastic bag, because you can use part of the contents for one meal and put the rest back in your freezer to serve later.

Commercial Processing

Vegetables for canning and freezing are grown particularly for that purpose. The canning or freezing plants are usually located in the vegetable production areas, so the harvested vegetables can be quickly brought to the plant for processing while fresh.

Canned and frozen vegetables are rich in minerals and vitamins because they are processed when at their best, and the processing preserves their nutritional value.

To begin with, the fresh vegetables are washed in large vats of continuously circulating water or under sprays of water. Most frozen vegetables are given a quick, partial cooking to protect them from changes that might occur during storage and cause undesirable odors and flavors. Potatoes, beets, carrots, and other vegetables that must be peeled are specially treated to remove the peel or are put through mechanical peelers. The stems of such vegetables as green beans are automatically snipped off by specially designed cutting machines.

The vegetables are then spread on moving belts that carry them to workers who do any extra peeling or cutting necessary and remove undesirable pieces. Some vegetables, such as peas, may also be sorted into sizes by special equipment. The end result of all this work is to bring the product up to the quality or grade desired.

Now the vegetables are filled into cans or packages and sometimes seasonings are added. The cans and packages are sealed automatically by high-speed machinery.

In the final processing of canned vegetables, the sealed cans are cooked under carefully controlled conditions of time and temperature and then quickly cooled. This is what insures the keeping quality of canned vegetables without refrigeration. (After the cans are opened the vegetables must, of course, be refrigerated if they are not for immediate use, but they need not be removed from the cans.)

In the final processing of frozen vegetables, the vegetables are quickly frozen in special low-temperature chambers.

In today's modern plants, most of the processing is done by automated equipment and there is little handling of the vegetables themselves by the plant workers. These high-speed processes bring us sanitary, wholesome products, preserved at the peak of their goodness and flavor.

Styles, Seasonings, and Sauces

Both canned and frozen vegetables are sold in many forms or styles. Beets, green beans, potatoes, and other vegetables may be found whole, cut, sliced, diced, and in other forms. Whole vegetables generally cost more than cut styles because it is hard to keep such fragile products as vegetables whole during processing.

Some vegetables, such as beets, are also sized when they are processed whole. This sizing also adds to the cost of the processed product, but whole vegetables of about the same size make an attractive serving, either hot or cold.

Fancy-cut vegetables, such as French-style green beans or julienne carrots (both French-style and julienne are sliced lengthwise) usually cost more than other cut styles and, because they are more attractive, are best used to dress up a dinner plate or cold salad.

Short-cut green beans, diced carrots, and tomato pieces are examples of the least expensive styles of processed vegetables, and the styles that are best used in soups and souffles.

Many frozen vegetables are available in butter sauces, with mushrooms, or other garnishes or flavorings. Some canned vegetables are also available in butter sauces or with other garnishes, such as tomatoes with green peppers and onions. Such vegetables, of course, cost more than the plain product, but let you serve something different without any extra work.

Tips on Containers

When you buy canned vegetables, be sure the cans are not leaking or swelled or bulged at either end. Bulging or swelling indicates spoilage. Small dents in cans do not harm the contents. Badly dented cans, however, should be avoided.

Packages of frozen vegetables should be firm. Because frozen vegetables should be used immediately after they have been defrosted—to avoid loss of quality, don't buy packages that are limp, wet, or sweating. These are signs that the vegetables have defrosted or are in the process of defrosting. Packages stained by the contents may have been defrosted and refrozen at some stage in the marketing process. The contents may be safe to eat, but refrozen vegetables will not normally taste as good as the freshly frozen vegetables.

Vegetables sold in glass jars with screw-on or vacuum-sealed lids are sealed tightly to preserve the contents. If there is any indication the lid has been tampered with, return the jar to the store and report the matter to the store manager.

A Consumer's Guide to Buying Canned and Frozen Vegetables

The grade and style of a vegetable, whether or not special seasonings or sauces are added—all affect the cost of the processed product and also determine the best way to serve the vegetable, so you get the most for your money and the most out of the vegetable.

Selecting the style, seasonings, and sauces is easy enough, because these are shown on the label. The grade or quality often is not indicated, but you can learn to tell differences in quality by trying different processors' or distributors' products.

To help you check the quality of canned and frozen vegetables you buy, the grades of some of the more popular vegetables are described in the list that follows, along with the styles of the vegetables.

Remember:

Grade A or Fancy vegetables, in whole or fancy-cut styles, are probably the most expensive vegetables. But they are the most tender and flavorful and make the most attractive servings for a special luncheon or dinner, either hot or in a cold salad.

Grade B or Extra Standard vegetables, in sliced or plain cut styles, are less expensive. They are good served hot or in casseroles or gelatin salads.

Grade C or Standard vegetables, diced or in pieces, are usually the least expensive vegetables. They are a good buy for use in soups, purees, or souffles.

All three grades of vegetables, in any style, are wholesome and nutritious. And tastes differ—most people like tender (Grade A) vegetables best, but some like more mature vegetables (Grades B or C).

Artichokes

Artichoke hearts—the tender inner part of the vegetable—are available frozen and canned. Artichoke hearts are also packed in vinegar and sauces, to be used like pickles or hors d'oeuvres. Canned whole artichokes are also available, and they may be served like the fresh vegetable. The repeated handpicking necessary to harvest artichokes makes it a relatively expensive vegetable.

Asparagus

Asparagus is more expensive than other vegetables because much of the harvesting and preparation during processing is done by hand. The spear or stalk consists of the stem and head (tip). There are two types of asparagus—green and white. Green asparagus is canned or frozen; white asparagus is canned. White asparagus is a delicacy, produced by mounding earth around the plant so that the stalk develops entirely underground. Sometimes canned asparagus is packed in glass jars, with a note on the label that color preservative (stannous chloride) has been added.

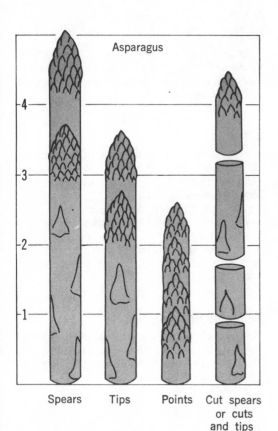

| Spears | Tips | Points | Cut spears or cuts and tips |

Beans, baked, kidney, and others

Many varieties of mature dry beans are processed by canning. Baked beans are processed in tomato sauce, or brown sugar and molasses, usually with pork, and cooked in ovens. Small white beans and lima beans are also available in tomato sauce, sometimes with a small amount of pork or meat flavoring. Red or kidney beans are prepared in a sweetened sauce or clear salt brine.

Top-quality mature dry beans have a smooth sauce and few broken or mashed beans are found in a can. Because of the unusually high protein content and food energy of these vegetables, they may be used as main dishes as well as side dishes or ingredients in salads.

Beans, green and wax

Called string beans before the development of stringless varieties, or snap beans, pole beans, or bush beans when they are fresh, the canned and frozen products are usually known as green beans and wax beans. Wax beans are so called because of their waxy yellow color. There is little difference in nutritional value of the two types of beans, but green beans are better known. "Blue Lake," a popular variety of green beans used for both canning and freezing, is often named on the can or package. Italian or "Romano" green beans are large flat beans.

Styles of both frozen and canned green and wax beans are: whole, French (julienne or shoe-string), and cut. Whole style beans are sometimes packed vertically in cans; when the beans are of about the same length, they can be labeled "whole asparagus style." French, julienne, or shoestring beans are sliced lengthwise. Cuts or "short cuts" are sliced crosswise. Beans cut diagonally are called "kitchen cuts" or "home cuts."

Beans, lima

Several types of lima beans are canned and frozen. The Fordhook variety, a name often shown on labels, is a large thick bean. Several varieties of lima beans have small, thin beans; these are usually called baby limas. Lima beans are white, yellow, or green, depending on their maturity when harvested. Each color has its own flavor. Green limas are usually the youngest beans.

Speckled butter beans are another variety of lima bean, found mostly in frozen form. They are larger than most other lima beans and have a different flavor. These beans range in color from green, pink, and red to lavendar and purple, with brown, purple, and other speckling.

U.S. Grade A and B lima beans are less starchy than Grade C, and baby limas are less starchy than the larger beans.

Beets

Canned beets are available whole, sliced, quartered, diced, and in strips. Beets prepared in a slightly thickened, sweet vinegar sauce are called Harvard beets.

Broccoli

Frozen broccoli is prepared as whole spears or stalks, short spears or florets (the head with a short portion of the stalk), broccoli cuts or pieces, and chopped broccoli.

The highest quality frozen broccoli looks much like the fresh vegetable—it has compact bud clusters that are dark green or sage green, sometimes with a decidedly purplish cast. Second quality broccoli may have slightly spread bud clusters.

Brussels sprouts

Brussels sprouts are a member of the cabbage family and they look like miniature cabbages. They get their name from Brussels, Belgium, the country where they originated.

Top quality frozen Brussels sprouts have tight-fitting leaves and are free from blemishes.

Cabbage

Sauerkraut is the only form of processed cabbage available in food stores. The shredded cabbage is fermented in a brine of its own juice and salt, and it may be flavored with peppers, pimientos, tomatoes, and various spices. It is available canned and in refrigerated packages, and at times, a semi-fresh product is sold from barrels or similar containers.

Carrots

Canned and frozen carrots are available whole, quartered, diced, as strips and round slices (cuts), and chips (frozen only). Canned small baby carrots are especially flavorful.

Cauliflower

Frozen cauliflower is separated into florets before it is frozen. Grade A cauliflower is white to creamy-white. Grade B often looks slightly gray or brown but turns white when cooked.

Corn

Processed sweet corn is found in many forms, styles, and grades. Canned corn may be cream style—with large or small pieces of kernels in a thick, creamy sauce prepared from corn, salt, sugar, water, and sometimes small amounts of starch; whole grain style, with the kernels generally whole and packed in a relatively clear liquid; and vacuum-pack whole grain, with kernels intact but little or no liquid. Most canned corn is prepared from yellow or golden-colored varieties, but some white corn also is canned. "Shoe peg" corn, a whole-grain white corn, has small, narrow kernels with a distinctive flavor.

Most frozen corn is whole-grain yellow or golden corn. A considerable amount is frozen on the cob.

Both canned and frozen corn may have peppers or pimientos or other foods added for flavor or appearance.

Much processed corn is packed according to U.S. grades, with the USDA grade mark on the label:

U.S. Grade A is tender and succulent, free from defects and has excellent flavor.

U.S. Grade B is slightly more mature and more chewy than grade A, reasonably free from defects, and has a good flavor.

U.S. Grade C is more mature and starchier than grades A and B but it is flavorful and nourishing.

Hominy

Hominy is prepared from the mature kernels of regular field corn. The kernels are soaked, cooked slightly, and then the hard outer covering is removed before further processing. Hominy is available in plastic bags in refrigerator cases, but it is usually canned, either in brine or as jellied hominy. It is a starchy vegetable like potatoes or sweet corn and is served hot. Jellied hominy may be sliced and fried like potato cakes.

Mushrooms

Mushrooms are canned in several styles: whole (including the stems), as buttons (the top only), sliced, and stems and pieces. They are sometimes processed in butter and broiled before they are canned. You may also find frozen mushrooms in some stores.

Okra

Sometimes called "gumbo," okra is quite popular in the Southern States. It is often used to flavor and thicken gumbos or thick soups. Since okra is now available canned and frozen, its use is spreading to other regions.

Small whole okra pods and pods cut into rings are available both canned and frozen. Canned fermented okra is partially fermented in a salt brine and has an acid, kraut-like flavor. Usually firm, with a bright green color, canned fermented okra may be served as a side dish, but it is usually used in soups or other foods. Small okra pods are also available pickled.

Onions

Whole onions are available both canned and frozen and breaded onion rings are available frozen. Canned whole onions are usually packed in a salt brine. Top-grade canned and frozen onions are specially selected for variety, size, and shape so that they will keep their good appearance during processing.

Peas, black-eye and other Southern varieties

Several varieties of peas are known as black-eye or Southern peas and sometimes by other names such as "creme" and "purple hull." These immature succulent peas are both canned and frozen. Sometimes a few "snaps"—tender pieces of the pod—are included with the peas for flavor or garnish. Some canned Southern peas are prepared from mature dry peas. These peas are somewhat starchy and have a different flavor.

Peas, green

Either canned or frozen, peas are one of the most popular processed vegetables. Different varieties are grown for the two methods of processing because of the different effects of canning and freezing on flavor and color. Two types of peas are used for canning—the smooth-skinned early or early June type, and the dimple-skinned or sweet type. Most peas for freezing are of the sweet type, especially developed for deep-green color.

U.S. Grade A or Fancy canned peas are tender and flavorful and their color is the typical soft pea-green. The juice is slightly green and water-like. Off-color peas are rarely found in a can.

U.S. Grade B or Extra Standard canned peas may be slightly mealy but they have a very good flavor. Their color may be variable and a few off-color peas or broken peas may be in a can. The liquid may be a slightly cloudy, light green.

U.S. Grade C or Standard canned peas tend to be mealy, and do not taste as sweet as Grades A and B. They are a dull pea-green and some blond or cream-colored or broken peas may be in a can. The liquid may be very cloudy with a starchy flavor.

Many canned early peas are sorted for size—tiny, small, medium small, medium large, large, or extra large. Sizes are often shown on the label. "Garden run" means no size separation has been made. "Assorted sizes" means two adjacent sizes. "Mixed sizes" means three or more sizes. "Sifted" means that some sizes have been removed. Sweet-type peas are not normally sorted for size.

Frozen peas are mostly larger and not as round as those used for canning. They are not usually sized, although a limited supply of excellent quality small round peas is frozen.

Peppers

Both green and red peppers are frozen whole, with or without stems, as well as halved, sliced, and diced. Frozen peppers are convenient to use for stuffing or as garnish. Red and green peppers are sometimes available canned too.

Potatoes

Processed white potatoes are available in many forms: Canned, small whole potatoes in salt brine; french-fried shoe strings vacuum-packed, ready to eat; frozen french fried in many sizes and shapes; frozen deep-fried small, whole potatoes, sliced or diced products, and patties or puffs made from mashed potatoes; and frozen, unfried products—ready-to-cook patties, or whole sliced, diced, or shredded potatoes. Most frozen french fries for home use are designed for finishing in the oven, though additional frying in deep fat or shallow fat produces good french fries.

Spinach
and other greens

Various leafy greens are available in canned or frozen form. Among them are: spinach, collards, kale, mustard, turnips (with or without immature roots), poke salad, endive, and Swiss chard. Spinach is processed in "whole leaf" and chopped styles, sometimes with various sauces and flavorings. The highest grade of these products is produced from young, tender plants.

Squash

Canned and frozen summer squash is prepared from small succulent squashes usually cut crossways. Several varieties are available, including the flavorful zucchini.

Canned and frozen winter squashes, very similar to pumpkin, are usually cooked and ready for use as a vegetable or in a pie filling.

Sweetpotatoes

Processed sweetpotatoes come in many forms, from only partially cooked to almost ready to eat. Canned sweetpotatoes may be vacuum-packed (without any liquid), in a sirup, or solid pack (tightly packed with little liquid). They are canned whole, mashed, or as pieces. Frozen sweetpotatoes are available whole or halved, peeled or unpeeled, baked, stuffed in a shell, sliced, french cut, diced, mashed, and sometimes formed into cakes.

Tomatoes

Canned tomatoes are usually peeled and packed in their own juice but they may have some added tomato pulp or semi-solid paste. The higher grades have a better color, usually more whole than broken pieces, and are practically free from peel, core, and other defects. U.S. Grade A Whole is a special grade, consisting principally of whole tomatoes.

Many canned tomato specialties, different from those you may usually buy, are becoming available. They include pear- or plum-shaped tomatoes, slices, dices, and other forms which are firm and have little juice. Many of these can be used in salads. Other specialties are: stewed tomatoes, which contain onion, pepper and other flavorful ingredients; tomatoes and okra; and tomatoes and hot peppers.

How to Buy
FRESH
FRUITS

Walk into today's food store and look at the luscious displays of fresh fruits available in fairly constant supply during the entire year.

This year-round abundance can be credited to the great strides made by growers, shippers and distributors—including improved varieties, more efficient methods of production, and advanced techniques of packaging, precooling, shipping, storing and refrigerated displaying of fruits.

GRADES FOR FRUIT

The Agricultural Marketing Service of the U.S. Department of Agriculture has established grade standards for most fresh fruits. These standards generally provide two or more grades which describe the quality of the fruit in a package. The top grade in most cases is either U.S. Fancy or U.S. No. 1. Official USDA standards define the quality each product should be to permit the USDA grade.

Use of USDA standards for grades is voluntary. Sometimes, however, under State or Federal regulations products must be graded and labeled on the basis of grade standards.

Most packers of fruits grade their products and some mark the containers with one of the established grades. If packages are so labeled, the packer is then legally obligated to make the contents measure up to official grade requirements. The shopper may purchase with a greater measure of confidence if he selects packages of fruit labeled with a grade.

Also, a few fruit dealers who pack consumer-size packages operate under the Federal or Federal-State continuous inspection service. This voluntary program—paid for by the dealer—provides for continuous inspection of the entire packing operation, including frequent inspection and grade analysis of the product. Products packed and certified under this service may be labeled with an official USDA grade shield or with one of the following statements "Packed Under Continuous Inspection of the U.S. Department of Agriculture" or "Packed By _____ Under Continuous Federal-State Inspection."

FOOD-BUYING TIPS

Do it yourself—There is no substitute for your own experience in choosing the right quality of fresh fruit for different uses. Tips in this booklet, however, can serve as a useful guide to achieving satisfaction and economy in your shopping.

Don't buy just because of low price—It seldom pays to buy perishable fruits merely because the price is low. Unless the lower price is a result of overabundance of the fruit at the time, the so-called bargain may be undesirable.

Buy only what you need—Modern home refrigeration makes it possible to keep an adequate supply of most perishable fruits on hand, but never buy more than you can properly refrigerate and use without waste—even if the product is cheaper in quantity.

Keep a lookout for deterioration—Even with the most modern handling methods, some products decline rapidly in quality while on display. Frequently such off-quality fruit can be bought at a reduced price, but the waste in preparation may offset the price reduction.

Don't buy on size alone—Large sized fruits are not necessarily the best quality, nor are they always economical. They may appear to be bargains, but may be entirely unsuited to the purpose you have in mind.

Appearance isn't everything—Select your fruit for best eating quality rather than outer appearance, if you want to shop economically. Appearance and quality are closely associated in many respects, but fine appearance does not always denote fine quality. Often a fruit with a very attractive appearance may have relatively poor eating quality because of a varietal characteristic or because of some internal condition such as overmaturity. On the other hand, a fruit with poor appearance due to poor color or superficial blemishes may have excellent eating quality.

Buy in season—Quality is usually higher, and prices more reasonable, when you buy fruit in season. Out-of-season produce is generally more expensive.

Shop for plentifuls—Through newspapers, radio, and television, the U.S. Department of Agriculture tells you each month which fruits are in greatest supply and worthy of your special attention. Such plentiful foods are usually good choices and reasonably priced.

Don't pinch!—Rough handling of fruits while you are selecting them causes spoilage and waste. Such loss to the grocer usually is passed on to the consumer, so your costs go up when fruit is carelessly handled. When you must handle a fruit to judge its quality, use thoughtful care to prevent injury.

A CONSUMER'S GUIDE
TO BUYING FRUIT

The following alphabetical list of fruits is designed as a reference to help you shop more intelligently. Some of the terms used (such as "mature" and "ripe") have special meanings in the produce field. A brief glossary on page 62 will help you understand these terms.

APPLES

The many varieties of apples differ widely in appearance, flesh characteristics, seasonal availability, and suitability for different uses.

For good eating as fresh fruit, the commonly available varieties are: Delicious, McIntosh, Stayman, Golden Delicious, Jonathan, and Winesap. For making pies and applesauce, use tart or slightly acid varieties such as Gravenstein, Grimes Golden, Jonathan, and Newtown.

For baking, the firmer-fleshed varieties—Rome Beauty, Northern Spy, Rhode Island Greening, Winesap, and York Imperial—are widely used.

Look for: Firm, crisp, well-colored apples. Flavor varies in apples and depends on the stage of maturity at the time the fruit is picked. Apples must be mature when picked to have a good flavor, texture, and storing ability. Immature apples lack color and are usually poor in flavor. They may have a shriveled appearance after being held in storage.

Most apples are marketed by grade, and many consumer packages show the variety, the grade, and the size. U.S. grades for apples are U.S. Extra Fancy, U.S. Fancy, U.S. No. 1, and combinations of these grades. U.S. No. 2 is a less desirable grade. Apples from the far western States are usually marketed under State grades which are similar to Federal grades. The qualities of color, maturity, and lack of defects—appearance in general—determine the grade.

Avoid: Overripe apples (indicated by a yielding to slight pressure on the skin and soft, mealy flesh) and apples affected by freeze (indicated by internal breakdown and bruised areas). Scald on apples (irregular shaped tan or brown areas) may not seriously affect the eating quality of the apple.

APRICOTS

Most fresh apricots are marketed in June and July, but a limited supply of imported apricots are available in the larger cities during December and January. Domestic apricots are grown principally in California, Washington, and Utah.

Apricots develop their flavor and sweetness on the tree, and should be mature—but firm—at the time they are picked.

Look for: Apricots that are plump and juicy looking, with a uniform, golden-orange color. Ripe apricots will yield to gentle pressure on the skin.

Avoid: Dull-looking, soft, or mushy fruit, and very firm, pale yellow, or greenish-yellow fruit. These are indications of overmaturity or immaturity respectively.

AVOCADOS

Avocados — grown in California and Florida— are available all year. Two general types and a number of varieties of each are grown. Depending upon type and variety, avocados vary greatly in shape, size and color. Most tend to be pear shaped, but some are almost spherical. Fruits weighing under one-half pound are most commonly available. Some have a rough or leathery textured skin, while others have a smooth skin. The skin color of most varieties is some shade of green, but certain varieties turn maroon, brown or purplish-black as they ripen.

Despite this variation in appearance, avocados are of good eating quality when they are properly ripened—becoming slightly soft. This ripening process normally takes from three to five days at room temperature, for the quite firm avocados usually found in the food store. Ripening can be slowed down by refrigeration.

Look for: For immediate use, slightly soft avocados which yield to a gentle pressure on the skin.

For use in a few days, firm fruits that do not yield to the squeeze test. Leave them at room temperature to ripen.

Irregular light brown markings are sometimes found on the outside skin. These markings have no effect on the flesh of the avocado.

Avoid: Avocados with dark sunken spots in irregular patches or cracked or broken surfaces. These are signs of decay.

An extra tip: When preparing avocados—to avoid the brownish color of avocado flesh when exposed to air—immediately place the peeled fruit in lemon juice until you are ready to use it.

BANANAS

Unlike most other fruits, bananas develop their best eating quality after they are harvested. This allows bananas to be shipped great distances, and almost our entire supply of bananas—available the year round—is imported from Central and South America. Bananas are sensitive to cool temperatures and will be injured in temperatures below 55 degrees. For this reason they should never be kept in the refrigerator. The ideal temperature for ripening bananas is between 60 and 70 degrees; higher temperatures cause them to ripen too rapidly.

Look for: Bananas which are firm, bright in appearance, and free from bruises or other injury. The stage of ripeness is indicated by the skin color: best eating quality has been reached when the solid yellow color is specked with brown. At this stage, the flesh is mellow and the flavor is fully developed. Bananas with green tips or with practically no yellow color have not developed their full flavor potential.

Avoid: Bruised fruit (which means rapid deterioration and waste); discolored skins (a sign of decay); a dull, grayish, aged appearance (showing the bananas have been exposed to cold and will not ripen properly).

Occasionally, the skin may be entirely brown and yet the flesh will still be in prime condition.

BLUEBERRIES

Fresh blueberries are on the market from May through September. Generally, the large berries are cultivated varieties and the smaller berries are the wild varieties.

Look for: A dark blue color with a silvery bloom, your best indication of quality. This silvery bloom is a natural, protective waxy coating. Buy blueberries that are plump, firm, uniform in size, dry, and free from stems or leaves.

CHERRIES

Excellent as dessert fruit, most sweet cherries found in the food store are produced in our Western States and are available from May through August. Red tart cherries —also called sour or pie cherries and used mainly in cooked desserts—have a softer flesh, lighter red color, and a tart flavor. They generally are shipped to processing plants and are sold frozen or canned.

Look for: A very dark color, your most important indication of good flavor and maturity in sweet cherries. Bing, Black Tartarian, Schmidt, Chapman, and Republican varieties should range from deep maroon or mahogany red to black, for richest flavor. Lambert cherries should be dark red. Good cherries have bright, glossy, plump-looking surfaces and fresh-looking stems.

Avoid: Overmature cherries lacking in flavor, indicated by shrivelling, dried stems, and a generally dull appearance. Decay is fairly common at times on sweet cherries, but because of the normal dark color, decayed areas are often inconspicuous. Soft, leaking flesh, brown discoloration, and mold growth are indications of decay.

CRANBERRIES

A number of varieties of fresh cranberries are marketed in large volume from September through January. They differ considerably in size and color, but are not identified by variety names in your food store.

Look for: Plump, firm berries with a lustrous color, for the best quality. Duller varieties should at least have some red color. Occassional soft, spongy, or leaky berries should be sorted out before cooking, because they may produce an off-flavor.

GRAPEFRUIT

Grapefruit is available all year, with most abundant supplies from January through May. While Florida is the major source of fresh grapefruit, there also is substantial production in Texas, California, and Arizona. Several varieties are marketed, but the principal distinction at retail is between those which are "seedless" (having few or no seeds) and the "seeded" type. Another distinction is color of flesh; white fleshed fruit is most common, but pink or red fleshed varieties are becoming increasingly available.

Grapefruit is picked "tree ripe" and is always ready to eat when you buy it in the store.

Look for: Firm, well-shaped fruits—heavy for their size, which are usually the best eating. Thin-skinned fruits have more juice than coarse-skinned ones. If a grapefruit is pointed at the stem end, it is likely to be thick-skinned. Rough, ridged, or wrinkled skin can also be an indication of thick skin, pulpiness, and lack of juice.

Grapefruit often has skin defects—such as scale, scars, thorn scratches, or discoloration—which usually do not affect the eating quality of the fruit.

Avoid: Soft, discolored areas on the peel at the stem end; water-soaked areas; loss of bright color, and soft and tender peel that breaks easily with finger pressure. These are all symptoms of decay—which has an objectionable effect on flavor.

GRAPES

Most table grapes available in food stores are of the European type, grown principally in California. Only small quantities of Eastern-grown American-type grapes are sold for table use.

European types are firm-fleshed and generally have high sugar content. Common varieties are Thompson seedless (an early green grape), Tokay and Cardinal (early bright red grapes), and Emperor (late, deep red grape). These all have excellent flavor when well matured.

American-type grapes have softer flesh and are more juicy than European types. The outstanding variety—for flavor—is the Concord, which is blue-black when fully matured. Delaware and Catawba are also popular.

Look for: Well colored, plump grapes that are firmly attached to the stem. White or green grapes are sweetest when the color has a yellowish cast or straw color, with a tinge of amber. Red varieties are better when good red predominates on all or most of the berries. Bunches are more likely to hold together if the stems are predominantly green and pliable.

Avoid: Soft or wrinkled grapes (showing effects of freezing or drying), grapes with bleached areas around the stem end (indicating injury and poor quality), and leaking berries (a sign of decay).

LEMONS

Most of the Nation's commercial lemon supply comes from California and Arizona, and is available the year round.

Look for: Lemons with a rich yellow color, reasonably smooth-textured skin with a slight gloss, and those which are firm and heavy. A pale or greenish yellow color means very fresh fruit with slightly higher acidity. Coarse or rough skin texture is a sign of thick skin and not much flesh.

Avoid: Lemons with a darker yellow or dull color, or with hardening or shriveling of the skin (signs of age), and those with soft spots, mold on the surface, and punctures of the skin (signs of decay).

LIMES

Most green limes sold at retail (sometimes called Persian or Tahitian limes) are produced in Florida and are marketed when mature. Imported limes are mostly the smaller yellow (or Key) lime.

Look for: Limes with glossy skin and heavy weight for the size.

Avoid: Limes with dull, dry skin (a sign of aging and loss of acid flavor), and those showing evidence of decay (soft spots, mold, and skin punctures).

Purplish or brownish irregular mottling of the outer skin surface is a condition called "scald," which in its early stages does not damage the flesh of the lime itself.

MELONS

Selection of melons for quality and flavor is difficult—challenging the skill of even the most experienced buyer. No absolute formula exists, but the use of several factors in judging a melon will increase the likelihood of success.

CANTALOUPS (Muskmelons)

Cantaloups, generally available from May through September, are produced principally in California, Arizona, and Texas, and some are imported early in the season.

Look for: The three major signs of full maturity —1. The stem should be gone, leaving a smooth, symmetrical, shallow basin called a "full slip." (If all or part of the stem base remains or if the stem scar is jagged or torn, the melon is probably not fully matured.) 2. The netting, or veining, should be thick, coarse, and corky—and should stand out in bold relief over some part of the surface. And 3. The skin color (ground color) between the netting should have changed from green to a yellowish-buff, yellowish gray, or pale yellow.

But also look for signs of ripeness, for a cantaloup might be mature, but not ripe. A ripe cantaloup will have a yellowish cast to the rind, have a pleasant cantaloup odor when held to the nose, and will yield slightly to light thumb pressure on the blossom end of the melon.

Most cantaloups are quite firm when freshly displayed in retail stores. While some may be ripe, most have not yet reached their best eating stage. Hold them for two to four days at room temperature to allow completion of ripening. After conditioning the melons, some people like to place them in the refrigerator for a few hours before serving.

Avoid: Overripeness, shown by a pronounced yellow rind color, a softening over the entire rind, and soft, watery, and insipid flesh. Small bruises normally will not hurt the fruit, but large bruised areas should be avoided, since they generally cause soft, watersoaked areas underneath the rind. Mold growth on the cantaloup—particularly in the stem scar, or if the tissue under the mold is soft and wet—is a sign of decay.

CASABA

This sweet, juicy melon is normally pumkin-shaped with a very slight tendency to be pointed at the stem end. It is not netted, but has shallow, irregular furrows running from stem end toward the blossom end. The rind is hard with a light green or yellow color. The stem does not separate from the melon, and must be cut in harvesting. The casaba melon season is from July to November; they are produced in California and Arizona.

Look for: Ripe melons with a gold yellow rind color and a slight softening at the blossom end. Casabas have no odor or aroma.

Avoid: Decayed melons, shown by dark, sunken water-soaked spots.

CRENSHAW

The large size and distinctive shape make this melon easy to identify. It is rounded at the blossom end and tends to be pointed at the stem end. The rind is relatively smooth with only very shallow lengthwise furrowing. The flesh is pale orange, juicy, and delicious—and generally considered outstanding in the melon family. Crenshaws are grown in California from July through October, with peak shipments in August and September.

Look for: These signs of ripeness—1. The rind should be generally a deep golden yellow, sometimes with small areas having a lighter shade of yellow. 2. The surface should yield slightly to moderate pressure of the thumb, particularly at the blossom end. 3. It should have a pleasant aroma.

Avoid: Slightly sunken, watersoaked areas on the rind (a sign of decay, which spreads quickly through the melon).

HONEY BALL

The honey ball melon is very similar to the honey dew melon, except that it is much smaller, is very round, and is slightly and irregularly netted over the surface. Use the same buying tips for this melon as for the honey dew melon.

HONEY DEW

The outstanding flavor characteristics of honey dews make them highly prized as a dessert. The melon is large (4 to 8 pounds), bluntly oval in shape, and generally very smooth with only occasional traces of surface netting. The rind is firm and ranges from creamy white to creamy yellow, depending on the stage of ripeness. The stem does not separate from the fruit, and must be cut for harvesting.

Honey dews are available to some extent almost all year round, due in part to imports during the winter and spring. Chief sources, however, are California, Arizona, and Texas—with the most abundant supplies available from July through October.

Look for: Maturity, shown by a soft, velvety feel, and for ripeness, shown by a slight softening at the blossom end, a faint pleasant fruit aroma, and a yellowish white to creamy rind color.

Avoid: Melons with a dead-white or greenish-white color and hard, smooth feel (which are signs of immaturity), large, watersoaked bruised areas (signs of injury), and cuts or punctures through the rind (which usually lead to decay). Small, superficial, sunken spots do not damage the melon for immediate use, but large decayed spots will.

PERSIAN

Persian melons resemble cantaloups, but are more nearly round, have finer netting, and are about the same size as honey dews. The flesh is thick, fine-textured, and orange colored. Grown primarily in California, they are available in fair supply in August and September.

Look for: The same factors of quality and ripeness listed for cantaloups.

WATERMELONS

Although watermelons are available to some degree from early May through September, peak supplies come in June, July, and August. Judging the quality of a watermelon is very difficult unless it is cut in half or quartered.

Look for: (in cut melons) Firm, juicy flesh with good red color, free from white streaks; seeds which are dark brown or black.

Avoid: Melons with pale colored flesh, and white streaks or "white heart," whitish seeds (indicating immaturity). Dry, mealy flesh or watery, stringy flesh are signs of overmaturity or aging after harvest.

If you want to buy an uncut watermelon, here are a few appearance factors which may be helpful (though not totally reliable) in guiding you to a satisfactory selection. The watermelon surface should be relatively smooth; the rind should have a slight dullness (neither shiny nor dull); the ends of the melon should be filled out and rounded; and the underside, or "belly," of the melon should have a creamy color.

NECTARINES

This fruit, available from June through September from California, combines characteristics of both the peach and the plum.

Look for: Rich color and plumpness and a slight softening along the "seam" of the nectarine. Most varieties have an orange-yellow color (ground color) between the red areas, but some varieties have a greenish ground color. Bright-looking fruits which are firm to moderately hard will probably ripen normally within two or three days at room temperature.

Avoid: Hard, dull fruits or slightly shriveled fruits (which may be immature—picked too soon —and of poor eating quality), and soft or overripe fruits or those with cracked or punctured skin or other signs of decay.

Russeting or staining of the skin may affect the appearance but not detract from the internal quality of the nectarine.

ORANGES

California, Florida, Texas, and Arizona produce our year-round supply of oranges.

Leading varieties from California and Arizona are the Washington Navel and the Valencia, both characterized by a rich orange skin color. The Navel orange, available from November until early May, has a thicker, somewhat more pebbled skin than the Valencia, the skin is more easily removed by hand, and the segments separate more readily. It is ideally suited for eating as whole fruit or as segments in salads. The western Valencia orange, available from late April through October, is excellent either for juicing or for slicing in salads.

Florida and Texas orange crops are marketed from early October until late June. Parson Brown and Hamlin are early varieties, while the Pineapple orange—an important, high-quality orange good for hand eating—is available from late November through March. Florida and Texas Valencias are marketed from late March through June. The Florida Temple orange is available from early December until early March. Somewhat like the California Navel, it peels easily, separates into segments readily, and has excellent flavor.

Oranges are required by strict State regulations to be well matured before being harvested and shipped out of the producing State. Thus skin color is not a reliable index of quality, and a greenish cast or green spots do not mean that the orange is immature. Often fully matured oranges will turn greenish (called "regreening") late in the marketing season. Some oranges are artificially colored to improve the appearance of the fruits. This practice has no effect on eating quality, but artificially colored fruits must be labeled "color added."

"Russeting" is often found on Florida and Texas oranges (but not on California oranges). This is a tan, brown, or blackish mottling or specking over the skin. It has no effect on eating quality, and in fact often occurs on oranges with thin skin and superior eating quality.

Look for: Firm and heavy oranges with fresh, bright-looking skin which is reasonably smooth for the variety.

Avoid: Light-weight oranges, which are likely to lack flesh content and juice. Very rough skin texture indicates abnormally thick skin and less flesh. Dull, dry skin and spongy texture indicate aging and deteriorated eating quality. Also avoid decay—shown by cuts or skin punctures, soft spots on the surface, and discolored, weakened areas of skin around the stem end or button.

PEACHES

A great many varieties of peaches are grown, but only an expert can distinguish one from another. These varieties fall into two general types: freestone (flesh readily separates from the pit) and clingstone (flesh clings tightly to the pit). Freestones are usually preferred for eating fresh or for freezing, while clingstones are used primarily for canning, although sometimes sold fresh.

Look for: Peaches which are fairly firm or becoming a trifle soft. The skin color between the red areas (ground color) should be yellow or at least creamy.

Avoid: Very firm or hard peaches with a distinctly green ground color, which are probably immature and won't ripen properly. Also avoid very soft fruits, which are overripe. Don't buy peaches with large flattened bruises (they'll have large areas of discolored flesh underneath) or peaches with any sign of decay. Decay starts as a pale tan spot which expands in a circle and gradually turns darker in color.

PEARS

Most popular variety of pear is the Bartlett, which is produced in great quantities (in California, Washington, and Oregon) both for canning and for sale as a fresh fruit. With the aid of cold storage, Bartlett pears are available from early August through November.

Several fall and winter varieties of pear are grown in Washington, Oregon, and California—and shipped to fresh fruit markets. These varieties—Anjou, Bosc, Winter Nellis, and Comice—keep well in cold storage and are available over a long period, from November until May.

Look for: Firm pears of all varieties. The color depends on variety. For Bartletts, look for a pale yellow to rich yellow color; Anjou or Comice—light green to yellowish green; Bosc—greenish yellow to brownish yellow (the brown cast is caused by skin russeting, a characteristic of the Bosc pear); Winter Nellis—medium to light green.

Pears which are hard when you find them in the food store will probably ripen if kept at room temperature, but it is wise to select pears that have already begun to soften—to be reasonably sure that they will ripen satisfactorily.

Avoid: Wilted or shriveled pears with dull-appearing skin and slight weakening of the flesh near the stem—which indicates immaturity. These pears will not ripen. Also avoid spots on the sides or blossom ends of the pear, which means that corky tissue may be underneath.

PINEAPPLES

Pineapples, which are available the year round but are at peak supply in April and May, come principally from Puerto Rico, Hawaii, and Mexico. Because pineapples must be picked when still hard (but mature), they must be allowed to ripen before they can be eaten. They will normally ripen within a few days at room temperature, but many are already ripe when you find them in the food store.

Look for: The proper color, the fragrant pineapple odor, a very slight separation of the eyes or pips, and the ease with which the "spike" or leaves can be pulled out from the top. Pineapples are usually dark green in mature hard stage. As the more popular varieties (such as Red Spanish and Smooth Cayenne) ripen, the green color fades and orange and yellow take its place. When fully ripe, the pineapples are golden yellow, orange yellow, or reddish brown—depending on the variety, although one seldom-seen pineapple (the Sugar Loaf) remains green even when ripe.

Also look for the maturity, shown by plump, glossy eyes or pips, firmness, a lively color, and fruits which are heavy for their size.

Avoid: Pineapples with sunken or slightly pointed pips, dull yellowish-green color, and dried appearance (all signs of immaturity). Also avoid bruised fruit—shown by discolored or soft spots—which are susceptible to decay. Other signs of decay (which spreads rapidly through the fruit) are: traces of mold, an unpleasant odor, and eyes which turn watery and darker in color.

PLUMS AND PRUNES

Quality characteristics for both are very similar and the same buying tips apply to both.

Plums—A number of varieties of plums are produced in California and are available from June to September. Varieties differ widely in appearance and flavor, so you should buy and taste one to see if that variety appeals to you.

Prunes—Only a few varieties of prunes are commonly marketed and they are all very similar. Prunes are purplish-black or bluish-black, with a moderately firm flesh which separates freely from the pit. Most commercial production is in the Northwestern States. Fresh prunes are available in food stores from August through October.

Look for: Plums and prunes with a good color for the variety, in a fairly firm to slightly soft stage of ripeness.

Avoid: Fruits with skin breaks, punctures, or brownish discoloration. Also avoid immature fruits (relatively hard, poorly colored, very tart, sometimes shriveled) and overmature fruits (excessively soft, possibly leaking or decaying).

RASPBERRIES, BOYSENBERRIES, ETC.

Blackberries, raspberries, dewberries, loganberries, and youngberries are similar in general structure. They differ from one another in shape or color, but quality factors are about the same for all.

Look for: A bright clean appearance and a uniform good color for the species. The individual small cells making up the berry should be plump and tender but not mushy. Look for berries that are fully ripened—with no attached stem caps.

Avoid: Leaky and moldy berries. You can usually spot them through the openings in ventilated plastic containers. Also look for wet or stained spots on wood or fiber containers, as possible signs of poor quality or spoiled berries.

STRAWBERRIES

First shipments of strawberries come from southern Florida in January, and then production increases, gradually spreading north and west into many parts of the country before tapering off in the fall. Strawberries are in best supply in May and June.

Look for: Berries with a full red color and a bright luster, firm flesh, and the cap stem still attached. The berries should be dry and clean, and usually medium to small strawberries have better eating quality than large ones.

Avoid: Berries with large uncolored areas or with large seedy areas (poor in flavor and texture), a dull shrunken appearance or softness (signs of overripeness or decay), or those with mold, which can spread rapidly from one berry to another.

Note: In most containers of strawberries you will likely find a few that are less desirable than others. Try to look at some of the berries down in the container to be sure that they are reasonably free from defects or decay.

TANGERINES

Florida is the chief source of tangerines. Considerable quantities of tangerines and similar types of oranges are produced in California and Arizona, some in Texas, and a few are imported. Tangerines are available from late November until early March, with peak supplies in December and January. The Murcott, a large, excellent variety of orange resembling the tangerine, is available from late February through April.

Look for: Deep yellow or orange color and a bright luster as your best sign of fresh, mature, good-flavored tangerines. Because of the typically loose nature of the tangerine skin, they will frequently not feel firm to the touch.

Avoid: Very pale yellow or greenish fruits, likely to be lacking in flavor (although small green areas on otherwise high-colored fruit are not bad) and tangerines with cut or punctured skins or very soft spots (all signs of decay, which spreads rapidly).

A CONSUMER'S GLOSSARY OF FRUIT TERMS

Blossom end—The opposite end from the stem end. The stem end will have a scar or remains of the stem to identify it. The blossom end is often more rounded than the stem end.

Breakdown of tissue—Decomposition or breaking down of cells due to pressure (bruise) or age (internal breakdown).

Decay—Decomposition of the fruit due to bacteria or fungus infection.

Ground color—The basic or background color of a fruit before the sun's rays cause the skin to redden. The ground color may be seen beneath and between the red blush of the fruit.

Hard—The terms "hard," "firm," and "soft" are subjective terms used to describe the degrees of maturity or ripeness of a fruit. A "hard" texture will not give when pressed. A "firm" texture will give slightly to pressure. A "soft" texture is, of course, soft to the touch. The term "mature green" is sometimes used instead of "hard."

Mature—Describes a fruit that is ready to be picked, whether or not it is ripe at this time. If a fruit is picked when mature, it is capable of ripening properly, but if picked when immature, it will not ripen properly.

Netting—The vein-like network of lines running randomly across the rind of some melons.

Ripe—Describes a fruit that is ready to be eaten.

Russeting—A lacy, brownish, blemish-type coating on top of the skin.

Scald—A blemish, or brownish discoloration, which occasionally develops in the skin of apples or other fruits in cold storage.

How to Buy CANNED and FROZEN FRUITS

By Elinore T. Greeley, Head,
Processed Products Standardization,
Fruit and Vegetable Division,
Agricultural Marketing Service.

Introduction

Canned and frozen fruits, preserved at the peak of goodness, are ready to serve as they come from the container and are delicious ingredients in salads, sauces, desserts, and other dishes. They are convenient to use and are always available.

Processed fruits differ in quality—taste, texture, and appearance—and are usually priced according to their quality.

Because different qualities of fruits are suited to different uses, you can make better buys by choosing processed fruits in the quality that fits your needs.

Grades

U.S. grade standards—measures of quality—have been established for most processed fruits by the U.S. Department of Agriculture's Agricultural Marketing Service.

U.S. Grade A **or** **Fancy**	Grade A fruits are the very best, with an excellent color and uniform size, weight, and shape. Having the proper ripeness and few or no blemishes, fruits of this grade are excellent to use for special purposes where appearance and flavor are important.
U.S. Grade B **or** **Choice**	Grade B fruits make up much of the fruits that are processed and are of very good quality. Only slightly less perfect than Grade A in color, uniformity, and texture, Grade B fruits have good flavor and are suitable for most uses.
U.S. Grade C **or** **Standard**	Grade C fruits may contain some broken and uneven pieces. While flavor may not be as sweet as in higher qualities, these fruits are still good and wholesome. They are useful where color and texture are not of great importance, such as in puddings, jams, and frozen desserts.

Many processors, wholesalers, buyers for food retailers, and others use the U.S. grade standards to establish the value of a product.

USDA also provides an inspection service which certifies the quality of processed fruits on the basis of these standards. A voluntary service, it is available for a fee. Under the continuous inspection program, processed fruits are inspected by highly trained specialists during all phases of preparation, processing, and packaging.

When a product has been officially graded under continuous USDA inspection, it may carry the official grade name and the statement "Packed under continuous inspection of the U.S. Department of Agriculture." The grade name and the statement may also appear within shields.

The grade name, such as "Fancy" or "Grade A," is sometimes shown without "U.S." in front of it. If the grade name alone appears on a container, the contents should meet the quality for the grade shown, even though the product has not been officially inspected for grade.

Progressive processors strive to maintain the quality of their products, so the brand name of a processed fruit may also indicate the quality. Sometimes stores will offer different qualities under different brands. Most processors pack fruits in at least two grades.

Labels

Federal regulations require that the following information be included on the front panel of the label of a can or package.

The common or usual name of the fruit.

The form (or style) of fruit, such as whole, slices, or halves. If the form is visible through the package, it need not be stated.

For some fruits, the variety or color.

Sirups, sugar, or liquid in which a fruit is packed must be listed near the name of the product.

The total contents (net weight) must be stated in ounces for containers holding 1 pound or less. From 1 pound to 4 pounds, weight must be given in both total ounces and pounds and ounces (or pounds and fractions of a pound).

The net weight of a product includes the sirup or liquid in which it is packed.

Other information required on the label, although not on the front panel, is:

- Ingredients, such as spices, flavoring, coloring, special sweeteners, if used.
- Any special type of treatment.
- The packer's or distributor's name and place of business.

Labels may also give the quality or grade, size, and maturity of the fruit, cooking directions, and recipes or serving ideas. If the label lists the number of servings in a container, the law requires that the size of the serving be given in common measures, such as ounces or cups.

You may find the USDA grade shield on cans or packages of fruits that have been packed under continuous USDA inspection.

Commercial Processing

Fruits for canning and freezing are harvested at the proper stage of ripeness so that a good texture and flavor may be preserved. Much of the processing is done by automated equipment and the fruits are handled little by plant workers. Present-day practices help assure us of wholesome, sanitary products with good flavor and quality.

The initial work in preparing canned and frozen fruits is similar. At the processing plant, the fresh fruits are usually sorted into sizes by machine and washed in continuously circulating water or under sprays of water. Some fruits, such as apples, pears, and pineapple, are mechanically peeled and cored. Next, they are moved on conveyor belts to plant workers who do any other peeling or cutting necessary. Pits and seeds are removed by automatic equipment, and the fruits are also prepared in the various styles—halves, slices, or pieces—by machine. Before the fruits are canned or frozen, plant workers remove any undesirable pieces.

Canned Fruits

Cans or glass jars are filled with fruit by semi-automatic machines. The containers are next moved to machines that fill them with the correct amount of sirup or liquid and then to equipment that automatically seals them. The sealed cans or jars are cooked under carefully controlled conditions of time and temperature to assure that the products will keep without refrigeration. After the cans or jars are cooled, they are stored in cool, dry, well-ventilated warehouses until they are shipped to market.

Frozen Fruits

Frozen fruits are most often packed with dry sugar. After the initial preparation, packages are filled with fruit by automatic equipment, sugar or sirup is added, and the containers are automatically sealed. The packaged fruit is then quickly frozen in special low-temperature chambers and stored at temperatures of 0° F. or lower.

Sizes and Servings

The size of a serving of processed fruits varies because of the different styles of fruits and the different ways of using them.

For fruit mixtures or small fruits that you might serve by measurement, one-half cup is the serving size commonly used for adults. Two halves are the usual amount of individual servings of fruit pieces.

The most popular can sizes and the average number of servings in them are:

Net Weight	Servings
8–8½ ounces – – – –	2
16–17 ounces – – – –	3–4
29 ounces – – – – –	7

The net weight shown on a label includes both fruit and sirup. For the best buy, figure out the cost per ounce. Large containers often cost less per ounce, but not always.

To figure the number of servings in packages of frozen fruits, consider the weight on the package as totally usable.

Storage

Proper storage is important in maintaining the quality of processed fruits.

If you keep **canned fruits** in a place no warmer than 75° F., they will usually retain their quality for a year or more. The color, flavor, and texture of canned fruits that have been stored at very warm temperatures or for long periods of time may not stay at top quality but the fruits still will be safe to eat. Once a can has been opened, the fruit should be refrigerated if it is not for immediate use.

Frozen fruits stored in an ice-cube compartment of a refrigerator usually will keep well for only a few days. If kept in a separate refrigerator-freezer compartment, most frozen fruits will keep satisfactorily for several weeks. To maintain the quality of frozen fruits for a longer time, store them in a freezer that can maintain a temperature of 0° F. or lower. If you wish to use only a portion of a package, be sure to replace the remaining portion in the freezer before it has thawed.

Tips on Containers

When buying **canned fruit,** avoid cans that show signs of bulging or swelling at the ends or of leakage. Small dents in a can will not harm the contents unless the dents have pierced the metal or loosened the can seam.

Fruits sold in glass jars with twist-off lids are tightly sealed to preserve the contents. If you find any indication that the lid has been tampered with, return the jar to the store and report it to the store manager.

Frozen fruits should be frozen solid. If fruits in a package are not firm, they may have lost quality. Avoid buying frozen fruit with stains on the package since this may indicate that the fruit was defrosted at some time during marketing. To insure the quality of frozen fruits, pick them up as the last item on your grocery shopping and take them home in an insulated bag.

A Consumer's Guide to Canned and Frozen Fruits

The grade, style, and sirup or special flavorings in which processed fruits are prepared all affect the cost of the fruits and how you may want to use them.

Most processed fruits are available in at least two grades. The grade is not often indicated on processed fruits, but you can learn to tell differences in quality by trying different brands. To help you choose the grade of fruit that will suit the use you have in mind, the grades of some of the most popular fruits are described in the list that follows, along with the styles in which the fruits are available.

You will find the style and the type of sirup or special packing on the label of processed fruits. Whole fruits or halves or slices of similar size are more expensive than mixed pieces of various sizes and shapes. You may choose among canned fruits packed in juice, special sweeteners, water, slightly sweetened water, and heavy or extra heavy sirup. The heavier the sirup, the sweeter and more flavorful the fruit, and sometimes the higher the price.

Remember:

Grade A (or Fancy) fruits are the most flavorful and attractive and therefore usually the most expensive. They are excellent to use for special luncheons or dinners, served as dessert, used in fruit plates, or broiled or baked to serve with meat entrees.

Grade B (or Choice) fruits, which are not quite as attractive or tasty as Grade A, are very good quality. They have many uses: as breakfast fruits, in gelatin molds, fruit cups or compotes, topping for ice cream, or as side dishes.

Grade C (or Standard) fruits vary more in taste and appearance than the higher grades and they cost less. They are useful in many dishes, especially where appearance is not important; for example, in sauces for meats, in cobblers, tarts, upside-down cake, frozen desserts, jam, or puddings.

Apples

Canned apples are available as slices and chunky pieces, packed in water, in a thickened, sweet and spicy sirup, or prepared with starch, sugar, and spices as pie filling mix. More expensive specialty packs are whole apples, cored like baked apples, with or without the peel, and artificially colored and spiced apple rings.

Applesauce

Applesauce, the most popular form of canned apples, is available in a chunky texture as well as the pureed form. It may also be spiced or combined with raspberries, strawberries, pineapple, apricots, or other fruits. Top quality applesauce is a bright color, and there is little separation of liquid from the sauce when it is removed from the container. Second quality applesauce

may be slightly thin or slightly stiff; separation of liquid from the sauce is more noticeable; and the color may be somewhat dull.

Apricots

Canned apricots are delectable just as they come from the can or jar. They also add a piquant flavor to sauces, salads, or baked goods. They are usually packed in heavy or extra heavy sirup. The styles most often found are unpeeled halves, unpeeled whole apricots, and peeled whole apricots, with or without the pits. Even in the higher grades, you may expect to find very small blemishes or "freckles" on unpeeled apricots. Peeled whole apricots, prepared from ripe, fleshy fruits, may sometimes be soft, and the pits may be loose.

Blackberries and similar berries

Several kinds of "cane" or "bush" berries are prepared as whole frozen berries, packed with or without sugar or sirup. Blackberries are the most common, but you may also find boysenberries, dewberries, loganberries, or youngberries.

Blueberries

A favorite for pie making, canned blueberries are sold as a ready-to-use pie filling mix, and they are also packed in water or light sirup.

Frozen blueberries are good as dessert by themselves or served with ice cream. Top quality frozen blueberries, with their bright blue-purple color, look much like the fresh berries.

HOW TO USE GRADES AND STYLES

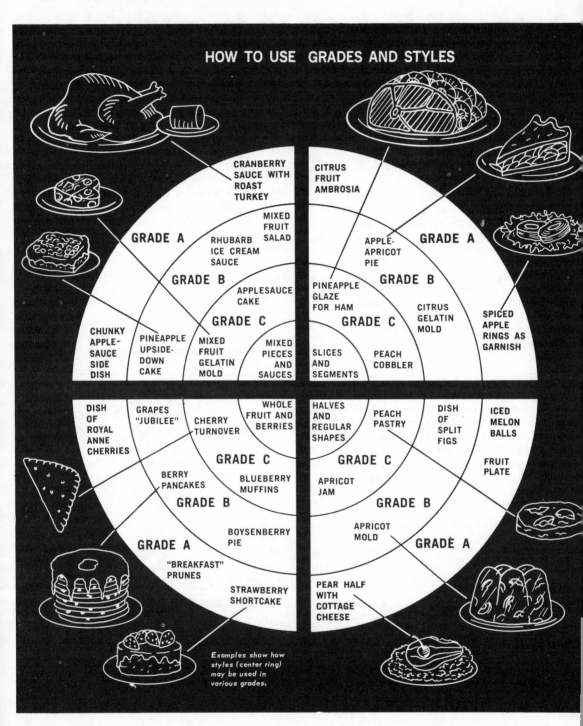

CRANBERRY SAUCE WITH ROAST TURKEY

CITRUS FRUIT AMBROSIA

MIXED FRUIT SALAD

GRADE A

RHUBARB ICE CREAM SAUCE

APPLE-APRICOT PIE

GRADE A

GRADE B

APPLESAUCE CAKE

PINEAPPLE GLAZE FOR HAM

GRADE B

CITRUS GELATIN MOLD

GRADE C

SPICED APPLE RINGS AS GARNISH

CHUNKY APPLE-SAUCE SIDE DISH

PINEAPPLE UPSIDE-DOWN CAKE

MIXED FRUIT GELATIN MOLD

MIXED PIECES AND SAUCES

SLICES AND SEGMENTS

GRADE C

PEACH COBBLER

DISH OF ROYAL ANNE CHERRIES

GRAPES "JUBILEE"

CHERRY TURNOVER

WHOLE FRUIT AND BERRIES

HALVES AND REGULAR SHAPES

PEACH PASTRY

DISH OF SPLIT FIGS

ICED MELON BALLS

GRADE C

GRADE C

FRUIT PLATE

BERRY PANCAKES

BLUEBERRY MUFFINS

APRICOT JAM

GRADE B

GRADE B

BOYSENBERRY PIE

APRICOT MOLD

GRADE A

GRADE A

"BREAKFAST" PRUNES

STRAWBERRY SHORTCAKE

PEAR HALF WITH COTTAGE CHEESE

Examples show how styles (center ring) may be used in various grades.

Cherries

Red tart cherries, sweet cherries, and maraschino cherries are the varieties you will find preserved by canning.

Red tart, or pie, cherries are pitted and packed in water or in a ready-to-use pie filling mix.

Sweet cherries are of two types, light and dark. Most light sweet cherries are the Royal Anne variety; usually they are not pitted, but some pitted light cherries are available. Light sweet cherries are often used as a side dish or in sauces. Dark sweet cherries usually are pitted; they are the variety used to make Cherries Jubilee.

Grade A sweet cherries are tender and thick-fleshed, about the same size, with few cracks or other blemishes. Light varieties are pinkish-yellow to pale amber with a very light pinkish tan or tannish brown blush. Dark varieties are deep red to purple red or purple black. Their colors are bright and uniform.

Grade B sweet cherries are thick fleshed but may be slightly soft and vary somewhat in size. The color of both light and dark varieties may be slightly dull.

Grade C sweet cherries are thin-fleshed and vary from firm to soft in texture. Some may be flabby. The size and color of both light and dark varieties are not as uniform as those in the higher grades.

Maraschino cherries are usually prepared from sweet cherries. They are artificially colored, and a specially flavored sirup gives them their distinctive taste. Often called cocktail cherries, they are very uniform in size, with pits removed, and are available with or without stems.

Cranberry Sauce

Canned cranberry sauce, a favorite to serve with chicken and turkey, is in jellied and whole-berry styles. Top quality cranberry sauce is a bright color, and the gel is tender. Whole-berry style contains whole berries and parts of berries.

Figs

This naturally sweet fruit, known from ancient times, is a delicious breakfast dish. Kadota figs, the most common pack, are light greenish-yellow to light amber. They are packed in sirup, most of which comes from the fruit itself. The better grades are always whole and practically uniform in size. Figs that are split or broken, usually because of over-ripeness, are of lower quality.

Other types, found less frequently, are the small Celeste and Mission varieties and "preserved" figs, which are packed in a very thick sirup.

Grapefruit and citrus mixtures

Grapefruit sections may be canned, frozen, or chilled. Mixed grapefruit and orange sections are available canned, and the two fruits are also sold as a chilled product in combination with pineapple pieces and whole maraschino cherries. When this combination is garnished with coconut, it is sometimes called "ambrosia fruits." In top quality packs, the citrus segments are firm and fleshy and at least three-fourths are whole. Canned grapefruit and orange sections are used as breakfast fruits or for salads.

Grapes

Canned grapes, usually of the Thompson seedless variety, are the same kind used in fruit cocktail. They can be used in desserts or gelatin salads. Dressed up with artificial colors and flavors, and sometimes spiced, they are often called "Grapes Jubilee."

Melon balls

Melon is one of the few fruits that normally is processed only by freezing. The most popular style is a mixture of honey dew melon and cantaloup balls.

Mixed fruits

Fruit Cocktail

Fruit cocktail, one of the best known canned fruit mixtures, contains five fruits: diced yellow peaches, diced pears, pineapple dices or tidbits, green-white seedless grapes, and red maraschino cherry halves. The mixture is one of a few standardized by Federal law to give a definite proportion of each of the fruits. Peaches and pears make up the greater part of the mixture.

Fruits for Salad

Carefully selected and almost always of Grade A quality, this canned mixture is a deluxe combination of fruits intended principally for making individual salads. Each can or jar contains approximately equal amounts of quarters or large slices of peaches and pears, apricot halves, large wedges of pineapple, and whole red maraschino cherries.

You can expect these numbers of servings (one piece of each kind of fruit in a serving) in these can sizes:

8 oz. – – – – **2 servings**
16 or 17 oz. – **3 servings of large pieces or 4 servings of small pieces**
29 or 30 oz. – **5 or 6 servings of large pieces or 7 servings of small pieces**

Also called salad fruit, this combination is usually packed in heavy or extra heavy sirup.

Tropical Fruit Salad

Various tropical and other fruits are used to make up this interesting canned fruit mixture. Check the label to see which fruits are included. The most common mixture consists of pieces of banana, pineapple, papaya, mango, passionfruit, and melon, packed in sweetened juices from passionfruit or other tropical fruits. Some mixtures contain mandarin orange sections, grapes, and maraschino cherries. The varying flavors and textures in tropical fruit salad make it an interesting and different combination to use in salads or fruit cups.

Other Mixed Fruits

Frozen mixed fruits are packaged in a wide range of fruit combinations. The usual pack consists of sliced peaches, dark sweet and red tart pitted cherries, blackberries, raspberries, and grapes. Because they are flavorful while still partially thawed, frozen mixed fruits are a quickly-prepared and elegant dessert. If a 10-ounce package is not large enough for a family, you can add sliced bananas, diced apples, mandarin oranges, or melon balls.

Less familiar than other fruit mixtures are canned mixtures of small dices and chips of peaches and pears, often with green-white seedless grapes added. These mixed fruits are a thrifty buy. They can be used in gelatin molds or as fruit cocktail.

Oranges

Most canned oranges sold in the United States are imported. Called mandarin oranges, they are packed as segments that are similar in shape and color to tangerine segments. Because they are naturally sweet, they are usually packed in water or light sirups. They are also available combined with pineapple segments or tidbits. Mandarin oranges have a variety of uses; they are excellent in gelatin molds and other salads and in fruit cups.

Peaches

Two types of canned peaches are available: clingstone and freestone. Clingstone peaches have a firm and smooth texture and clean-cut edges. Freestone peaches have a softer texture and raggedy edges. Both kinds are yellow to yellow-orange, except for the seldom-seen white freestone.

Both types come in these styles: whole (usually

spiced), halves, slices, quarters, and mixed pieces of irregular sizes and shapes. Once in a while you may find diced peaches, but dices are usually packed in canned fruit cocktail and other fruit mixes.

Canned peaches are packed in light, heavy, or extra heavy sirups, water, or slightly sweetened water.

Frozen peaches are usually sliced for easy-to-serve dishes. They are also packed in frozen mixed fruits.

Pears

Canned pears may be found as halves, slices, or quarters, and mixed pieces of irregular sizes and shapes. Sometimes the variety, such as Bartlett, will be on the label. Pears as dices and chips are used in fruit cocktail and other mixed fruits.

Top quality, Grade A, pear halves, quarters, and slices have an almost translucent, very light color. They neither vary much in size or shape nor have a lot of trimmings or broken pieces. In this grade, canned pears may have only a few slight blemishes and rarely have any pieces of stem, peel, or core. They also have a tender, even texture, with no graininess or breakdown of flesh.

Grade B canned pears are slightly less perfect than Grade A but are still of very good quality. In Grade B, the texture may have moderate graininess. In thrifty Grade C, you will find more blemishes, greater variation in shapes, and more broken pieces.

Mixed pieces of irregular sizes and shapes are always Grade B or Grade C because they lack uniformity of shape and vary in texture. But pear pieces are often very good in other respects.

Whole pears usually come colored and spiced. They usually rate Grade A because they are specially selected as to size, freedom from blemishes, and proper ripeness.

Canned pears are packed in light, heavy, or extra heavy sirups and in water, slightly sweetened water, or juices.

Pears are not available frozen.

Pineapple

Hawaii supplies us with most of our processed pineapple products. Puerto Rico, Mexico, and other countries also ship to the United States. Because pineapple varieties are not the same in each producing area, slight color and flavor differences are normal.

Canned pineapple is prepared by special cutting machines to give almost perfect-sized slices and other forms. You will find 10 whole, cored slices in a 20-ounce can and 8 slices in a 30-ounce can. (The larger can holds slices which are both larger in diameter and thicker.) There are also special flat cans containing 4 to 5 slices.

Other popular and versatile forms are crushed pineapple, tidbits, and chunks or large cube-like pieces. Special styles include whole, cored cylinders and spears. All of these styles are most often of very high quality. Half slices and broken slices do not rate as high because of appearance.

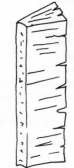

Frozen pineapple is available in a limited number of forms, mostly tidbits, chunks, and crushed. Often these are garnished with mint or mint flavoring.

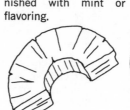
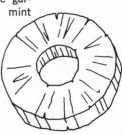

Plums

Two principal types of plums are canned. Purple plums (or prune-plums) are readily available, while the green-yellow plums (sometimes called Green Gage or Yellow Egg) are not always in stores. Purple plums usually are not peeled; green-yellow plums are. Ordinarily neither type is pitted. As with other fruits, plums are packed in sirups of different sweetness.

Prunes

Dried prunes in cans or glass jars are ready to serve. Packed in their own juice, they are known as "Prepared Prunes" or "Breakfast Prunes."

Raspberries

Both red and black raspberries are frozen and canned. Because raspberries are so delicate, you can expect some slightly crushed berries even in high quality packs.

Frozen red raspberries are usually packed in a sugar sirup. Handle them carefully and follow package directions closely to keep these berries plump and fresh looking.

Rhubarb

Grown for its edible stalk, rhubarb is not really a fruit but is used as one. Rarely canned, but frozen with a high proportion of sugar, rhubarb must be cooked before use. Before cooking, its color will be pinkish to green.

Strawberries

A year-round favorite, frozen strawberries can be purchased whole, sugared or unsugared. They are also available as slices or halves with sugar added. When thawed, the sugar melts with the natural juices of the strawberries to form a sirup.

Frozen strawberries come in a wide range of packaging: whole berries loose in large see-through bags and all styles in cups, cartons, or special fiber-metal cans. Quick-thaw pouches (which can be placed in warm water) make it possible to use the berries almost immediately.

In packages of Grade A frozen strawberries, a high proportion are well-colored red berries or slices. Whole berries are reasonably firm, not seedy, and have only a few blemishes, stems, or pieces of caps. Grade A sliced berries are equally as good although there will be a few mushy portions. Slicing and subsequent freezing often cause mushiness of the riper berries.

Grade B frozen strawberries are less colorful with more pinkish berries or slices.

Only limited amounts of strawberries are canned, but canned strawberry pie fillings are seen more and more often in stores. Because strawberries become pale during canning, these products are often artificially colored. If so, the label will name the artificial coloring as well as other ingredients.

How to Buy BEEF ROASTS & BEEF STEAKS

USDA CHOICE

Whether it's for pleasing a family, delighting dinner guests, or stretching the food budget, the versatile beef roast is a favorite choice of home-makers across the country.

There are many kinds of beef roasts ranging from rib roasts, the gourmet's delight, to arm pot roasts, for hearty he-man meals. Each of these cuts can vary in quality, depending upon the kind of carcass from which it came, but all are nutritious and all can provide good eating if properly prepared. The secret lies in suiting the cooking method to the grade and the cut you select.

A tender, juicy steak is a mealtime favorite of millions of Americans. To make sure that **your** steak will be tender and juicy, you need to know something about both buying the beef and cooking it.

Many different cuts of beef are called "steaks" —and any one of these cuts can vary in quality, depending upon the kind of carcass from which it came. But all are nutritious and all can provide good eating if properly prepared. The secret lies in suiting the cooking method to the grade and the cut you select.

About Beef Quality

Beef varies in quality more than any other kind of meat. But you don't have to learn to judge beef quality for yourself. USDA grades are a reliable guide to meat quality—its tenderness, juiciness, and flavor. The grades are based on nationally uniform Federal standards of quality and are applied by USDA graders. Therefore, you can be sure that a USDA Choice porterhouse steak, for example, will provide the same good eating no matter where or when you buy it.

How Beef is Graded

Meat grading is a voluntary service provided by USDA's Agricultural Marketing Service to meat packers and others who request it and pay a fee for the service. So not all meat is graded, although a large percentage of it is.

USDA graders, who are highly trained in meat quality, grade only whole carcasses or wholesale cuts. This is because quality differences are difficult, or impossible, to recognize in the smaller retail cuts. When the carcass is graded, a shield-shaped grademark containing the letters USDA and the grade name—such as Prime, Choice, or Good—is applied with a roller-stamp. The grade shield is rolled on, in a long ribbon-like imprint, all along the length of the carcass and across both shoulders. Then when the carcass is divided into retail cuts, one or more of the grademarks will appear on most of these cuts.

Only meat which has first passed a strict inspection for wholesomeness may be graded. So you may be sure when you see the grademark that the meat came from a healthy animal and was processed in a sanitary plant.

Inspection for Wholesomeness

All meat processed in plants which sell their products across State lines must, under Federal law, be inspected for wholesomeness. This service is another provided by the U.S. Department of Agriculture. USDA meat inspectors also supervise the cleanliness and operating procedures of meat packing plants to assure that meat is not contaminated or adulterated.

Meat which passes the USDA inspection for wholesomeness is stamped with a round mark which bears the legend "U.S. INSP'D & P'S'D." This mark is placed only once on wholesale cuts. So you are likely to see it only on large cuts of meat—seldom on steaks. Packaged meat foods, however, such as frozen dinners and canned meats, are required to carry the inspection mark on the label if they are to be sold in interstate commerce.

Learn to recognize both the inspection mark— a circle—and the grademark—a shield. Remember they mean different things. The inspection mark tells you that the meat is **clean** and **wholesome**. The grademark tells you the **quality** of the meat.

LOOK FOR THE GRADE

Each USDA beef grade is a measure of a distinct level of quality. Because beef can vary so much in quality, it takes eight grades to span the range. The lower three grades—USDA Utility, Cutter, and Canner—are seldom, if ever, sold as retail cuts. They go mostly into ground beef or into processed meat items such as hot dogs.

The grade most widely sold at retail is USDA Choice. Choice grade is produced in the greatest volume and retailers have found that this level of quality pleases most of their customers. Some stores, however, offer two grades—Prime and Choice or Choice and Standard, for example—so that their customers may have a choice of quality and price.

Pictured here are rib roasts and Porterhouse steaks in each of the first five grades, together with a description of the level of quality that can be expected in each of those grades.

 USDA PRIME

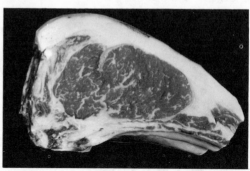

Prime grade beef is the ultimate in tenderness, juiciness, and flavor. It has abundant marbling— flecks of fat within the lean—which enhances both flavor and juiciness. A U.S. Prime rib roast is considered by many as the finest meat dish available. Prime round, rump, and sirloin tip roasts also provide excellent eating. Prime grade roasts are the best for dry-heat (oven) cooking.

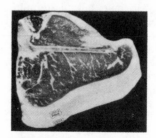

Steaks of this grade are the best for broiling.

USDA CHOICE   **USDA GOOD**

USDA Choice rib, rump, round, and sirloin tip roasts can also, like Prime, be oven roasted. They will be quite tender, juicy, and flavorful. Choice grade beef has slightly less marbling than Prime, but still is of very high quality.

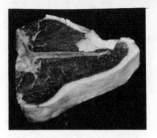

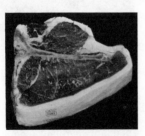

Most USDA Choice steaks are good for broiling and pan-broiling, too — they will be very tender, juicy, and flavorful.

Good grade beef often pleases thrifty shoppers because it is somewhat more lean than the higher grades. It is relatively tender, but because it has less marbling it lacks some of the juiciness and flavor of the higher grades. Some stores sell this quality of beef under a "house" brand name rather than under the USDA grade name.

USDA STANDARD

 USDA COMMERCIAL

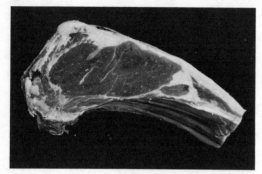

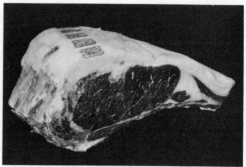

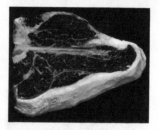

Standard grade beef has a high proportion of lean meat and very little fat. Because it comes from young animals, beef of this grade is fairly tender. But because it lacks marbling, it is mild in flavor and most cuts will be somewhat dry unless prepared with moist heat.

Commercial grade beef is produced only from mature animals—the top four grades are restricted to young animals. It has abundant marbling (compare it with the Prime grade above), and will have the rich, full flavor characteristic of mature beef. However, Commercial grade beef requires long, slow cooking with moist heat to make it tender. When prepared in this manner it can provide delicious and economical meat dishes.

BEEF CHART

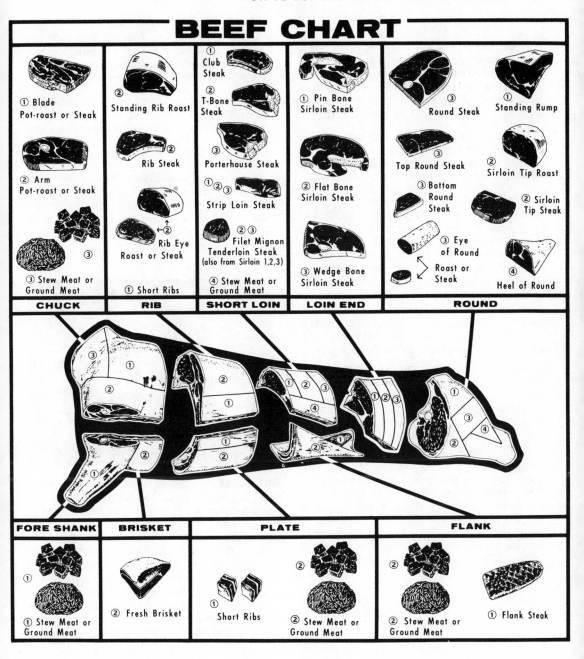

CHUCK

① Blade
Pot-roast or Steak

② Arm
Pot-roast or Steak

③ Stew Meat or
Ground Meat

RIB

Standing Rib Roast

Rib Steak

Rib Eye
Roast or Steak

① Short Ribs

SHORT LOIN

① Club
Steak

② T-Bone
Steak

③ Porterhouse Steak

①②③ Strip Loin Steak

②③ Filet Mignon
Tenderloin Steak
(also from Sirloin 1,2,3)

④ Stew Meat or
Ground Meat

LOIN END

① Pin Bone
Sirloin Steak

② Flat Bone
Sirloin Steak

③ Wedge Bone
Sirloin Steak

ROUND

③ Round Steak

① Standing Rump

③ Top Round Steak

② Sirloin Tip Roast

③ Bottom
Round
Steak

② Sirloin
Tip Steak

③ Eye
of Round
Roast or
Steak

④ Heel of Round

FORE SHANK

① Stew Meat or
Ground Meat

BRISKET

② Fresh Brisket

PLATE

① Short Ribs

② Stew Meat or
Ground Meat

FLANK

② Stew Meat or
Ground Meat

① Flank Steak

LOOK FOR THE CUT

Regardless of their quality grade, some cuts of beef are naturally more tender than others. Cuts from the less-used muscles along the back of the animal—the rib and loin sections—will always be more tender than those from the active muscles such as the shoulder (chuck), flank, and round.

The most tender cuts make up only a small proportion of the beef carcass—and they are in greatest demand. Therefore, they command a higher price than other cuts.

Names given beef cuts sometimes vary from store to store and in different parts of the country. It would be impossible to try to list them all here. Moreover, the terms used do not always mean the same thing. For example, a "cross cut rib roast" may be cut from the blade portion of the chuck in some places—in others it may be from the shoulder arm portion of the chuck. It is not the cut from the rib roast, as you might assume from the name. A "Delmonico" steak is cut from the ribeye in some parts of the country, while in other areas it is cut from the chuck.

Chuck cuts probably get more variation in terminology than any other. Some names "coined" for steaks cut from the chuck and used in various parts of the country include California, Western, Cheyenne, petite butter, finger, breakfast, his 'n hers—and there are many more.

The best guide in identifying beef cuts is the standard terminology shown in the following pages and generally recognized throughout the meat industry. Many stores, fortunately, do employ these terms in identifying the meat cuts they sell. The kind of bone in a cut also helps in identifying it. The T-bone and rib bone, for example, indicate tender cuts, while a round bone, such as in the arm chuck, means a less tender cut.

The beef cuts illustrated are the most widely sold and widely known. Together with each picture is a descripton of the cut, suggested cooking methods for it in various grades, and approximate amounts you'll need to buy per serving.

Buy any beef roast you intend to cook with dry heat (oven roasting) big enough—at least 4 pounds—to keep it from overcooking, especially if you want to serve some of it rare or medium rare.

For greatest eating satisfaction, buy any steak you intend to broil at least one inch thick. For example, if you like medium-rare steak, you'll find it difficult to achieve this degree of "doneness" with a thin steak.

RIB ROAST—Unexcelled for tenderness and flavor, easy to prepare, carve, and serve, this is the favorite for company fare. It can be oven-roasted in the top four grades but for maximum tenderness, juiciness, and flavor select USDA Prime or Choice. Because it has a rather large proportion of bone and fat, you will need to allow at least one-half a pound of rib roast per person. For company meals, you may wish to allow up to a pound per person. Buy it at least two ribs thick for proper cooking. Frequently called: Standing rib or prime rib (even though not graded USDA Prime).

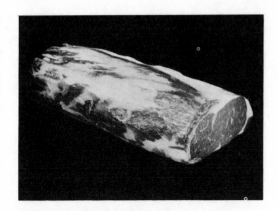

RIBEYE ROAST—The meaty, boneless heart of the standing rib, this cut has excellent flavor and is superbly tender in the higher grades. Like the standing rib, from which it is cut, it can be oven-roasted in Prime through Standard grades. Allow a third of a pound per person.

SIRLOIN TIP—This is a boneless roast, with very little waste. Despite its name, it is not as tender as a sirloin steak. But it has good flavor and in Prime, Choice, and Good grades is tender enough to be oven-roasted. Pot roast lower grades. Allow at least a third of a pound per person. Also frequently called: loin tip, round tip, knuckle.

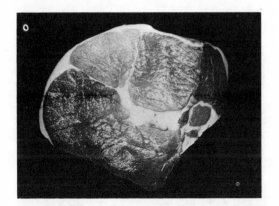

RUMP ROAST—This is a very flavorful cut, but it is less tender than the rib and it also contains a considerable amount of bone. In Prime, Choice, and Good grades, it can be oven-roasted; pot roast the lower grades. The rump is often sold boned and rolled, for easier carving. Allow at least a half-pound of bone-in rump per person and about a third of a pound per person for boneless rump.

EYE-OF-ROUND ROAST—Lean and meaty, this less-tender cut has good flavor. It may be oven-roasted in Prime and Choice grades but should be pot roasted in lower grades. Allow at least a third of a pound per person.

HEEL OF ROUND—A boneless, less-tender cut from the round, this roast contains several muscles, of varying tenderness. It should be pot roasted regardless of grade. Allow at least one-third of a pound per person.

SHOULDER ARM—Contains less bone than the blade chuck, but this cut is less tender. It has the same well-developed flavor, however. Pot roast in all grades. Allow about one-half of a pound per person.
Also called: round bone chuck or arm roast.

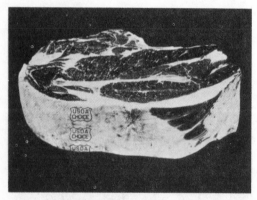

BLADE CHUCK—An economical roast, with excellent, full beef flavor, this one can be oven-roasted in the Prime and Choice grades, although it has several muscles that vary in tenderness. All grades make excellent pot roast. You'll need about three-fourths of a pound per person.

SHOULDER CLOD—This is a meaty cut from the outside of the chuck. It has a well-developed flavor, and no bone. A fairly tender cut, it may be oven-roasted in the Prime, Choice, and Good grades. Pot roast lower grades. Allow one-third of a pound, or more, per person.

TENDERLOIN (FILET MIGNON) — The most tender of all steaks, the tenderloin has no bone and very little fat. Broil or pan-broil it in all grades. Allow about 6 to 8 ounces per person.

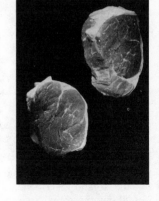

BRISKET—Often cured and sold as corned beef, the brisket is also sold fresh, usually with bones removed. Definitely a less tender cut, it must be cooked with moist heat (pot roasted) in all grades. Allow at least one-half of a pound per person.

PORTERHOUSE — Often considered the best steak, the porterhouse usually sells at a higher price than other bone-in steaks. It has a generous section of tenderloin, which can be removed and served separately as filet mignon. Broil or pan-broil in Prime, Choice, and Good grades. Porterhouse is a good steak for special occasions — and for such events allow 12 to 16 ounces per person.

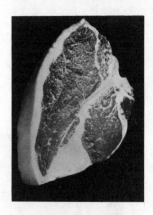

T-BONE—Very similar to the porterhouse steak, but with a smaller amount of tenderloin, the T-bone can be used in the same fashion. Broil or pan-broil it in Prime, Choice, and Good grades. For generous servings, allow 12 to 16 ounces per person.

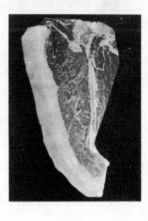

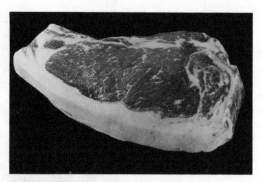

CLUB STEAK—The club steak, like the porter-house and the T-bone, is cut from the short loin. It has the same large muscle as the porterhouse and the T-bone, but has no tenderloin. Its rela-tively small size makes this steak well suited to individual servings. Allow 12 to 14 ounces per person. Rib steaks are often sold as club steaks since they, too, contain the same large muscle.

SIRLOIN—The sirloin is a large steak, which makes it suitable for family or party fare. It con-tains several different muscles and varies in size, shape, and bone size. To get the most for your money, look for one with a small amount of bone (wedge or round bone); but for maximum tender-ness, pick out a sirloin with a long, flat bone. Sirloins are frequently cut into two boneless steaks—top sirloin and bottom sirloin. The top sirloin is the better of the two. Broil or pan-broil in Prime, Choice, and Good grades; braise in lower grades. For bone-in sirloins allow 8 to 10 ounces per person depending on amount of bone.

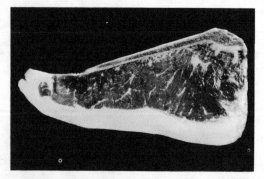

STRIP LOIN STEAK—This steak is the same as the large muscle in both the porterhouse and the T-bone. It is a very flavorful, tender steak which may be broiled or pan-broiled in the Prime, Choice, and Good grades. Allow 12 to 14 ounces per person. This steak is also sold boneless—in which case, allow 10 to 12 ounces per person. The strip loin steak is often sold in restaurants as a New York Strip steak or a Kansas City steak.

SIRLOIN TIP—This is a boneless steak, less tender than the regular sirloin. Can be broiled or pan-broiled in Prime and Choice grades. Braise in lower grades. Allow 6 to 8 ounces per person.

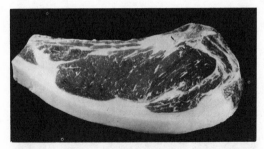

RIB—This steak is cut from the rib section, and includes the rib bone. It is sold as rib roast when cut two or more ribs thick. It has a well-developed flavor and is very tender; broil or pan-broil in Prime, Choice, and Good grades. Allow 12 to ˙ ˙ ounces per person. Often called a club steak.

RIBEYE—Cut from the eye of beef rib, this steak is boneless, and has little fat. Like the rib steak, it has a well-developed flavor and is **very** tender. Broil or pan-broil in Prime, Choice, and Good grades. Allow 8 to 10 ounces per person. The ribeye steak is often called a Delmonico stea

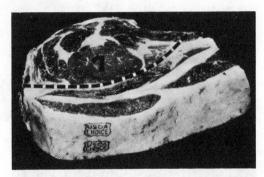

BLADE CHUCK—This is an economical steak, with a well-developed flavor, but it varies in tenderness. The "first cut" of blade chuck (shown in the picture) is the one adjacent to the rib roast and contains a sizable extension of the ribeye muscle—identified in the picture by the number "1". In the Prime, Choice, and Good grades, this portion may be cut out and broiled—it will make a delicious and tender steak. Other sections of this cut are definitely less tender and should be cooked with moist heat (braised), as should Prime and Choice chuck steaks which are not "first cuts" and all lower grades of chuck steaks. Allow about 10 to 12 ounces per serving. Stores sometimes cut small boneless steaks from the blade chuck region and give them varied names.

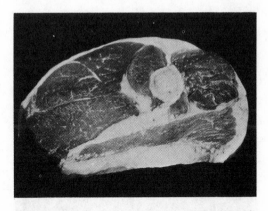

ARM CHUCK—Sold as steak in some stores, this cut is best used as Swiss steak or braised. It is definitely a less-tender cut, but it has a well-developed flavor. It can be identified by the round arm bone. It has very little waste; allow about 6 to 8 ounces per person. Also called: Arm steak.

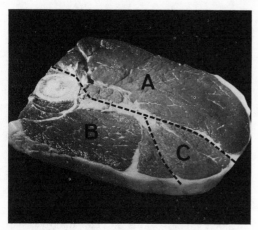

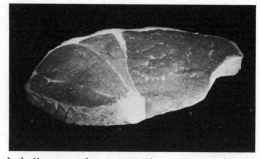

ROUND—Because it has very little waste, the round steak is usually an economical buy. It is not as flavorful and juicy as some of the other steaks because it lacks marbling. The full round contains three muscles which vary in tenderness. It can be divided as shown.

b. bottom round—not as tender as top; cook with moist heat in all grades.
Also called outside round, bottom round is often sold with the eye-of-the-round attached.

c. eye-of-round — also a less tender cut, but when sliced thin, Prime and Choice grades can be pan-broiled; cook with moist heat in other grades.
Allow about 6 to 8 ounces per person for any of these round steaks.

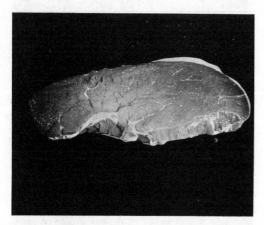

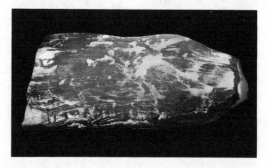

a. top round—the tenderest of the three muscles, can be broiled or pan-broiled in Prime and Choice grades; braise the lower grades.
Also called inside round.

FLANK—Boneless steak, with very little fat. Definitely a less-tender cut, but it has a well-developed flavor. Braise, cook with moist heat, in any grade. Allow 6 to 8 ounces per person. Many restaurants list flank steak on the menu as "London Broil."

How to Buy POULTRY

LOOK FOR THE USDA SHIELD—

● It tells you:

● You may find it on:

the grade
or quality
of the
poultry

the poultry label

or a

wing tag

The official grade shield certifies that the poultry has been graded for quality by a technically trained government grader. The grading service is provided on a voluntary basis to poultry processors and others who request and pay a fee for it.

Federal-State Graded

When grading is done in cooperation with a State, the official grade shield may include the words "Federal-State Graded."

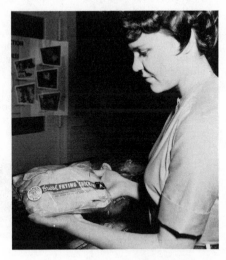

A USDA grader checks poultry for quality.

When selecting poultry, wise consumers look for the grade shield—assurance of the quality.

SELECT BY GRADE (QUALITY)

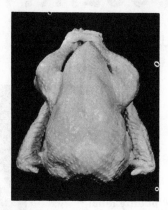
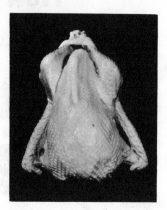

The highest quality is U.S. Grade A. Grade A birds are
- fully fleshed and meaty
- well finished
- attractive in appearance

Grade B birds may be:
- less attractive in finish and appearance.
- slightly lacking in meatiness

Grade B is seldom printed on poultry labels.

U.S. grades apply to five kinds of poultry: chicken, turkey, duck, goose, and guinea.

Poultry must be officially inspected for wholesomeness before it can be graded for quality. Often, the inspection mark and the grade shield are displayed together, as shown.

You may find the grade shield on any kind of chilled or frozen, ready-to-cook poultry or poultry parts (including chicken, turkey, duck, etc.).

INSPECTION MARK   GRADE MARK

**Mark
of wholesomeness**   **Mark
of quality**

The wing-tag also may include the class name—in this case, "Frying Chicken."

SELECT BY CLASS

The grade of the poultry does not indicate how tender the bird is—the age (class) of the bird is the determining factor.

Young birds are more tender than older ones.

If the poultry is not young, the label will carry the words—"mature," "old," or similar words as indicated under the mature classes below.

Young tender-meated classes are most suitable for barbecuing, frying, broiling, or roasting:

- Young chickens may be labeled—young chicken, Rock Cornish game hen, broiler, fryer, roaster, or capon.

- Young turkeys may be labeled—young turkey, fryer-roaster, young hen, or young tom.

- Young ducks may be labeled—duckling, young duckling, broiler duckling, fryer duckling, or roaster duckling.

Mature, less-tender meated classes may be preferred for stewing, baking, soups, or salads.

- Mature chickens may be labeled—mature chicken, old chicken, hen, stewing chicken, or fowl.

- Mature turkeys may be labeled—mature turkey, yearling turkey, or old turkey.

- Mature ducks, geese, and guineas may be labeled—mature or old.

POULTRY TIPS

- Chilled or frozen ready-to-cook poultry may be purchased in various sizes and forms to suit every occasion.

- Most kinds of ready-to-cook poultry are available as parts and in whole, halved, and quartered form. Some kinds are also available as boneless roasts and rolls.

- All poultry is perishable. Care and cleanliness should be used in the preparation, cooking, and serving of poultry products.

- Keep frozen poultry hard-frozen until time to thaw, and cook promptly after thawing.

- Use fresh-chilled poultry within 1 to 2 days.

- Completely cook poultry at one time. Never partially cook, then store, and finish cooking at a later date.

- Left-over cooked poultry, broth, stuffing, and gravy should be separated, covered, and refrigerated. Use within 1 to 2 days. Freeze for longer storage.

- Serve poultry often—it is a nutritious, delicious taste-treat the year around!

How to Buy LAMB

By Sandra Brookover,
Consumer Meat Specialist; Livestock Division,
Agricultural Marketing Service

Versatility never had it so good!

Today's lamb means zesty flavors and serving possibilities that challenge the imagination. Shish kabobs impaled over the barbecue, sizzling lamb chops, roasted leg of lamb, bubbling lamb stew—lamb is today's word for good eating!

Because lamb is from animals usually less than one year old, it is a tender and delicately flavored meat. This tenderness rates lamb a high degree of kitchen "workability" (most cuts may be cooked by the dry-heat method and are best when served hot).

Nutrition, too, has its role in lamb's popularity. One serving of lamb will provide the average adult with significant quantities of vitamin B-1, vitamin B-2, iron and niacin.

The large variety of lamb cuts available today opens up a world of tempting and attractive serving suggestions. It is the purpose of "How to Buy Lamb" to guide you in selecting these cuts according to quality grade and your serving needs. Then proper preparation, which is also discussed, will be your personal tribute to lamb's natural delicacy and flavorful tenderness.

ABOUT LAMB QUALITY

Today's lamb is a quality product for the quality-conscious. It does vary to some extent in its generally high quality level, but you don't have to learn to judge that quality for yourself. USDA grades are a reliable guide to lamb quality—its tenderness, juiciness, and flavor. The grades are based on nationally uniform Federal standards of quality and are applied by USDA graders. Therefore, you can be sure that USDA Choice lamb chops, for example, will provide the same good eating no matter where or when you buy them.

In addition to lamb, USDA also has grades for yearling mutton (meat from animals one to two years old) and mutton (over two years). Graded yearling mutton and mutton are seldom found, however, in retail stores.

ABOUT LAMB YIELD

USDA also grades lamb for yield. The yield grades measure the ratio of lean meat to fat and bone. They are based on a rating system of five—with Yield Grade 1 representing the highest yield of lean meat, and Yield Grade 5 the lowest.

Variations in the yield result primarily from the differences in fatness on the outside of the carcass and in fat deposited on the inside of the carcass. If you buy a carcass or wholesale cuts of lamb for your freezer, you should be aware that there are considerable differences in the meat yield between carcasses in the same quality grade, and take this into consideration in arriving at the carcass price you should pay. The pictures below, of two lamb rib chops, illustrate an extreme variation in the proportion of lean which results from differences in the amount of fat covering. Based on retail prices of lamb in early 1971, there was a value difference between carcasses of adjacent yield grades of nearly 4 cents per pound.

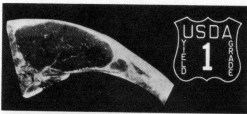

LAMB CHART

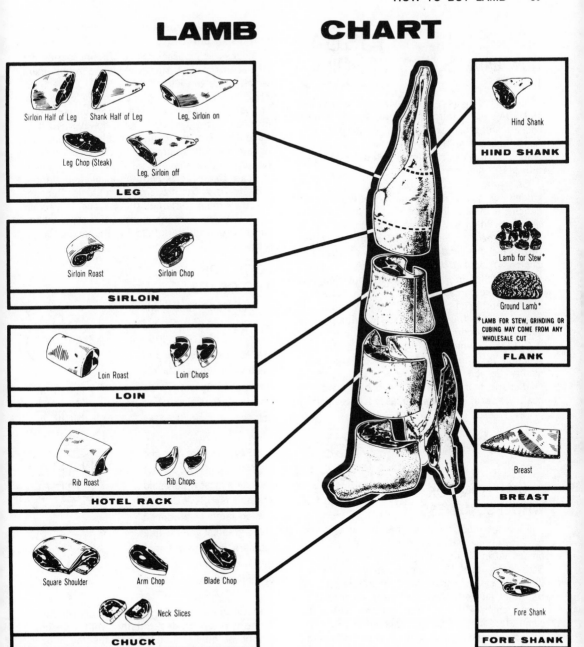

LEG
Sirloin Half of Leg   Shank Half of Leg   Leg, Sirloin on
Leg Chop (Steak)   Leg, Sirloin off

SIRLOIN
Sirloin Roast   Sirloin Chop

LOIN
Loin Roast   Loin Chops

HOTEL RACK
Rib Roast   Rib Chops

CHUCK
Square Shoulder   Arm Chop   Blade Chop
Neck Slices

HIND SHANK
Hind Shank

FLANK
Lamb for Stew*
Ground Lamb*
*LAMB FOR STEW, GRINDING OR CUBING MAY COME FROM ANY WHOLESALE CUT

BREAST
Breast

FORE SHANK
Fore Shank

HOW LAMB IS GRADED

Meat grading is a voluntary service provided by USDA's Agricultural Marketing Service to meat packers and others who request it and pay for it. Approximately two thirds of all lamb produced is graded for quality. The grading is done by highly trained USDA graders.

Only whole carcasses or wholesale cuts are graded for quality since quality differences are difficult or next-to-impossible to recognize in retail cuts. When the carcass is graded, a purple shield-shaped grademark containing the letters USDA and the grade name—such as Prime or Choice—is applied with a roller-stamp. The grade shield is rolled in a ribbon-like imprint along the length of the carcass and across both shoulders. Then when the carcass is divided into retail cuts, one or more of the grademarks should appear on most of these cuts.

Only lamb which has first passed a strict inspection for wholesomeness may be **graded for quality.** So you may be sure when you see the grademark that the meat also came from a healthy animal and was processed in a sanitary plant.

INSPECTION FOR WHOLESOMENESS

All meat must be inspected for wholesomeness, by either State or Federal inspectors. Meat processed in plants selling their products across State lines must be federally inspected to see that it is clean, wholesome, unadulterated, and truthfully labeled. However, meat processed in plants which sell their products only within the same State may be State inspected in any State having an inspection system equal to the Federal. Otherwise, such meat must be federally in-

spected. Federal inspection is another service provided by USDA.

Meat which passes the USDA inspection for wholesomeness is stamped with a round mark which bears the legend "U.S. INSP'D. & P'S'D." This mark is placed only once on wholesale cuts, so that you are likely to see it only on large cuts of meat. Packaged meat foods, however, such as frozen dinners and canned meats, that are sold in interstate commerce, carry the USDA inspection mark on the label.

Learn to recognize both the inspection mark—a circle—and the grademark—a shield. Remember they mean different things. The inspection mark tells you that the meat is **clean** and **wholesome.** The grademark tells you the **quality** of the meat.

LOOK FOR THE GRADE

Each USDA lamb grade is a measure of a distinct level of quality. Five grades span the range of quality — Prime, Choice, Good, Utility, and Cull. The two lower grades are seldom, if ever, sold as retail cuts.

USDA Prime is the highest quality grade, but the grade most widely sold at retail is USDA Choice. Choice lamb is produced in the greatest volume and retailers have found that this quality pleases most of their customers.

Pictured on the next page are lamb rib chops in the two top grades, together with a description of the quality that can be expected in each of these grades.

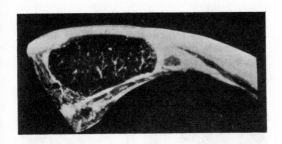

USDA PRIME

Prime grade lamb is very tender, juicy, and flavorful. It has generous marbling—flecks of fat within the lean—which enhances both flavor and juiciness. Prime chops and roasts are excellent for dry-heat cooking—broiling and roasting. Prime grade lamb is not carried widely at the retail level.

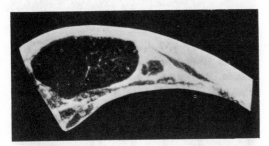

USDA CHOICE

Choice grade lamb has slightly less marbling than Prime, but still is of very high quality. Like Prime, Choice chops and roasts are very tender, juicy and flavorful and are suited to dry-heat cooking.

LOOK FOR THE CUT

Regardless of their quality grade, some cuts of lamb are naturally more tender than others. Cuts from the less-used muscles along the back of the animal—the rib and loin sections—will always be more tender than those from the active muscles such as the shoulder, flank, and leg.

The most tender cuts make up only a small proportion of the lamb carcass—and they are in greatest demand. Therefore, they command a slightly higher price than other cuts.

Consistently tender lamb cuts include the sirloin chop or steak, the loin chop, loin roast, rib chop, and rib roast. You will find that most cuts of USDA Prime and Choice lamb—including shoulder cuts—are tender and can be oven roasted, broiled, or pan-broiled. A leg of lamb graded Choice or Prime, for example, is a delicate delight when oven roasted.

The less tender cuts—the breast, riblets, neck, and shanks—can be braised slowly to make excellent (and tender!) lamb dishes.

The best way to identify lamb cuts is with the standard terminology shown on the following pages. These terms are generally recognized throughout the meat industry.

Illustrated on the following pages are the most widely sold and widely known retail cuts of lamb, along with descriptions of the cuts and suggested cooking methods.

RETAIL LAMB CUTS

RIB CHOPS Cut from the rib (rack), these tender chops (on the left in photo) are delicious broiled, pan-broiled, or panfried. For best results, have rib chops cut **at least** 1 inch in thickness. Approximate cooking time for 1 inch—12 minutes; 1½ inches—18 minutes; and 2 inches—22 minutes.

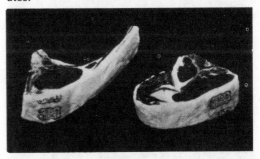

LOIN CHOPS One of the most popular of lamb cuts, loin chops (on the right in photo), can be easily identified by the T-bone. These chops are delicious when broiled, pan-broiled or panfried. Cooking time is the same as for rib chops.

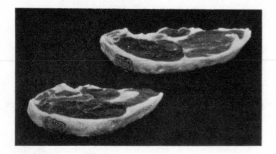

SIRLOIN STEAKS or **CHOPS**   Cut from the sirloin section of the lamb leg, these chops can also be broiled, pan-broiled, or panfried. Follow cooking suggestions given for rib and loin chops.

LEG OF LAMB

Since the leg of lamb is often too big to fully use, sirloin chops can be cut from the sirloin section of the roast, and the remaining portion prepared as an oven roast.

The **French-style leg** has a small amount of meat trimmed from the end of the shank, and the exposed bone can be decorated after roasting.

The **American-style leg** differs from the French-style in that the shank bone has been removed and the shank meat folded back into a pocket on the inside and fastened with skewers.

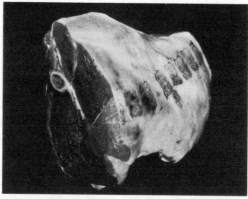

The **sirloin half**/leg of lamb (butt half) is the upper half of the leg—usually with the sirloin on. This cut makes a delicious oven roast.

The **shank** or lower half of the leg (see identification chart) is often merchandised separately. It is sometimes sold at a slightly higher price than the butt half because it yields more meat. Whenever the shank and butt are sold at the same price, the shank half of the leg is the better value.

For **any** leg roast weighing 5-8 pounds, allow approximately 35 minutes per pound in a 325° F. oven. The meat thermometer reading will be 175-180° when the roast is done.

RIB ROAST This cut is the section used for making rib chops. In wholesale terms, the rib roast cut is called the "rack."

You can fashion the rack into a "French roast" by removing about 1½ inches of meat from the ends of the ribs. Then after roasting, cover rib ends with paper frills for a decorative touch.

The elegant "crown roast" is made with at least two rib roasts (racks), with the back bone removed, shaped into a crown and secured with twine. Ends of the ribs are trimmed so that they can be decorated like the French roast.

Any of these roasts, which are all fashioned from the same basic cut, are perfect for oven roasting. A rib or crown roast weighing 4-6 pounds (put in a 325° F. oven) will require approximately 35 minutes per pound cooking time. Your meat thermometer will read 175 to 180° when the roast is done.

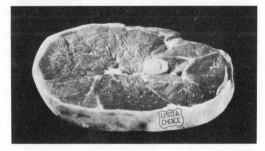

LEG STEAK Leg steaks are lean meaty slices cut from the center area of the leg, and are easily identified by the round leg bone. This cut is suitable for broiling, pan-broiling, or panfrying.

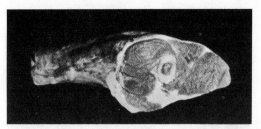

SHANKS Economical and best prepared by simmering in liquid or braising, lamb shanks are also nutritious! Shank sections are delicious, too, in lamb stew. If prepared by braising, shanks will require approximately 1½ to 2 hours total cooking time.

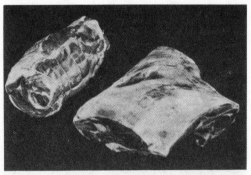

SHOULDER ROAST (Square-Cut and Boned and Rolled) The square-cut shoulder roast (on right in photo), identified easily by the arm and blade bones, is considered an economical cut of lamb.

The boned shoulder roast (on the left) is convenient to serve, and is commonly sold at retail as illustrated here—boned, rolled and tied. A boneless shoulder can also be fashioned into a cushion shoulder roast for stuffing.

Both shoulder roasts are suitable for oven roasting (preferably at a low temperature of 325° F., at 35-45 minutes per pound) OR suitable for braising (slowly browned and cooked with a small amount of liquid added). Cook to an internal temperature of 175-180°, as indicated by your meat thermometer.

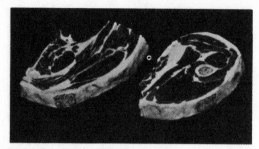

BLADE or **ARM SHOULDER CHOPS**   These cuts (from the shoulder roast) are fine for broiling, pan-broiling or panfrying. Preferably, for best results in cooking, they should be at least 1 inch thick. To broil a 1-inch chop requires a total cooking time of approximately 12 minutes.

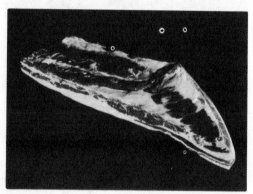

BREAST   The breast contains the rib bones and breast bone and is considered an economical buy. Often this cut is boned and rolled or boned for stuffing. A nice variation is to include fruit or vegetables in the stuffing. A less tender cut, the breast should be prepared by braising or simmering in liquid. When braising at a moderate oven temperature of 325° F., a boned and rolled breast roast requires 1½ to 2 hours total cooking time.

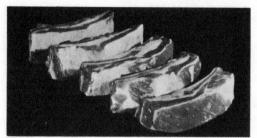

RIBLETS   These economy lamb cuts are made from the breast by cutting between the rib bones. They are best prepared by braising (requiring an approximate total cooking time of 1½ to 2 hours) or simmering in liquid. They are also delicious when cooked over charcoal on the outdoor grill.

***SHISH KEBABS**   Shish kebabs are cubes of boneless lamb usually cut from the shoulder or leg and skewered. They may be found pre-threaded on wooden skewers in some retail stores or the lamb cubes may be sold in bulk. A favorite way to prepare lamb shish kebabs is to marinate the cubes for a period of several hours, then put them on long skewers to charcoal broil or oven broil.

***GROUND LAMB**   Boneless lamb from the neck, breast, shanks and flank is generally used in making ground lamb. However, any part can be boned and ground. The ground lamb is best prepared as patties for broiling, pan-broiling, or panfrying—OR—as a lamb loaf for oven roasting.

* Not illustrated.

A FEW VARIATIONS

Although the above terms are quite standard, the names given lamb cuts do vary among stores and restaurants in different parts of the country. It would be impossible to list all of the variations here, but some terms are known in the trade.

These include: the **English chop,** a double loin lamb chop; **lamb cutlets,** meat from the lamb leg cut similar to round steak in beef; **crown roast of lamb,** the "sovereign" of the lamb kingdom, a formal-looking cut from the rack or rib area; **rack of lamb,** usually a restaurant menu item for two, from the rib; and **Saratoga chops,** boneless lamb chops from the inside shoulder muscles.

How to Buy MEAT FOR YOUR FREEZER

"Can I save money by buying a side of beef?"

This, and similar questions, are often asked by owners of home freezers. There is no easy "yes" or "no" answer. The answer can be found only by making a careful comparison of costs among the alternatives available to you.

Basically, you have three alternatives in buying meat for your freezer: buying a whole carcass, side, or quarter; buying wholesale cuts (loin, round, chuck, etc.); or buying retail cuts.

It is the purpose of this bulletin to help you compare the costs under these alternatives, and also to point out a number of other factors that you should consider. The information provided is intended primarily to answer the questions most frequently asked by consumer-buyers—those relating to costs, grades, kinds of cuts, and yields of usable meat.

POINTS TO CONSIDER

Wholesomeness . . . quality . . . how much to buy . . . cost . . . convenience . . . service . . . and getting good value for your money . . . these are all factors you should take into account in buying meat for your freezer.

You should also consider the amount of meat you can store in your freezer, the amount your family can use within a reasonable time, and the kinds of cuts and quality your family prefers. And you should be aware of the kinds and quantity of the various cuts that you get from a carcass or wholesale cut.

As in any buying situation, success in buying meat for your freezer depends upon your knowledge of what you are purchasing.

Carcass, Side, or Quarter

When you buy a whole carcass or side (half a carcass, including both fore and hind quarters), you will get a wide variety—the entire range of cuts, both high- and low-priced. These will include some you might not normally buy, such as the brisket, short ribs, and shank. But most locker and freezer provisioners, who specialize in preparing meat for the freezer, will convert cuts that you do not want to use "as is" into ground meat or stew meat. In addition, they will usually age meat to the extent desired and will cut it to your order.

A carcass, side or quarter is normally sold by its "hanging" or gross weight. This means the weight before cutting and trimming. The amount of usable meat you take home will, of course, be considerably less—how much less can vary substantially.

For a beef carcass, cutting loss (bone, fat trim, shrink, etc.) could vary from 20 to 30 percent or more. A 25-percent cutting loss, which is not unusual, means that a 300-pound side of beef would yield 225 pounds of usable meat cuts.

A rule of thumb for carcass beef is: 25 percent waste, 25 percent ground beef and stew meat, 25 percent steaks, and 25 percent roasts. Not all of the steaks and roasts, however, are from the loin and rib, the most tender portions. The table on page 96 will give you a good idea of the typical yield from a beef carcass or side.

Buying a quarter involves many of the considerations already mentioned. In addition, you should be aware of the difference in the kinds of cuts you get from a hindquarter as compared with a forequarter.

A hindquarter of beef will yield more steaks and roasts, but will cost more per pound than a forequarter. In 1967 and 1968, this difference in price averaged about 17 cents a pound. A forequarter of beef, while containing the delectable rib roast, has more of the less-tender cuts than the hindquarter. The chuck, or shoulder, makes up about one-half of the forequarter's weight. The yield of usable lean meat, however, is greater in the forequarter than in the hindquarter.

APPROXIMATE YIELDS FROM WHOLESALE CUTS OF BEEF
(300 LB. SIDE, YIELD GRADE 3)

	% of Wholesale Cut	Pounds
Round (68 lbs.)		
Round Steak	39.7	27.0
Rump Roast (Boneless)	14.6	9.9
Lean Trim	17.9	12.2
Waste (fat, bone, and shrinkage)	27.8	18.9
Total Round	100.0	68.0
Trimmed Loin (50 lbs.)*		
Porterhouse, T-Bone, Club Steaks	30.6	15.3
Sirloin Steak	49.8	24.9
Lean Trim	6.4	3.2
Waste (fat, bone, and shrinkage)	13.2	6.6
Total Loin	100.0	50.0

* Does not include Kidney knob and flank.

	% of Wholesale Cut	Pounds
Rib (27 lbs.)		
Rib Roast (7″ cut)	67.8	18.3
Lean Trim	12.6	3.4
Waste (fat, bone, and shrinkage)	19.6	5.3
Total Rib	100.0	27.0
Square-Cut Chuck (81 lbs.)		
Blade Chuck Roast	33.0	26.7
Arm Chuck Roast (Boneless)	21.5	17.4
Lean Trim	25.9	21.0
Waste (fat, bone, and shrinkage)	19.6	15.9
Total Chuck	100.0	81.0

APPROXIMATE YIELDS OF CUTS FROM BEEF QUARTERS
(300 LB. SIDE, YIELD GRADE 3)

	% of Quarter	Pounds
Hindquarter (144 lbs.)		
Round Steak	18.8	27.0
Rump Roast (Boneless)	6.9	9.9
Porterhouse, T-Bone, Club Steaks	10.6	15.3
Sirloin Steak	17.3	24.9
Flank Steak	1.0	1.5
Lean Trim	14.6	21.0
Kidney	.6	.9
Waste (fat, bone, and shrinkage)	30.2	43.5
Total hindquarter	100.0	144.0
Forequarter (156 lbs.)		
Rib Roast (7″ cut)	11.7	18.3
Blade Chuck Roast	17.1	26.7
Arm Chuck Roast (Boneless)	11.2	17.4
Brisket (Boneless)	4.0	6.3
Lean Trim	31.6	49.2
Waste (fat, bone, and shrinkage)	24.4	38.1
Total forequarter	100.0	156.0

Wholesale cuts

If you don't want all of the cuts that come with a side or quarter, or if your freezer space is limited, you might consider buying wholesale cuts. For example, you might buy a beef short loin, from which you will get porterhouse, T-bone, and club steaks, plus some ground beef or stew meat; a whole pork loin, for pork loin roasts and chops; or a leg of lamb, for several leg chops or steaks and a roast.

Consult the carcass charts on the following pages to see the kinds of retail cuts that come from the various wholesale cuts.

Wholesale cuts usually are bought from locker and freezer provisioners and others who sell meat as sides or quarters although sometimes they can be bought at a supermarket.

Retail cuts

A third alternative open to freezer owners is buying at retail only the particular cuts you prefer. By watching for advertised "specials" on these cuts, you can often save money.

This method of buying, of course, also enables you to buy as little, or as much, of a particular cut as you desire—and to control the amount of money you spend at one time. Buying a side or quarter of beef is a rather large investment—and if you must "finance" this purchase, you should include any interest charges when comparing the costs of alternative methods of buying.

But remember, also, that retail cuts usually must be rewrapped for long-term freezer storage—and the cost of this wrapping paper or foil should be taken into account.

See page 107 for a discussion of the importance of proper wrapping and freezing.

How Carcass and Wholesale Cut Prices Compare

If you plan to buy a forequarter or hindquarter, or wholesale cuts, you should have some idea of how each of these is normally priced in relation to carcass prices. The tabulation below shows average New York carlot-volume prices for USDA Choice steer beef as reported by the USDA Livestock Market News Service for 1968. These price relationships will vary considerably during the year, however, due to differences in demand. For example, during 1968, when there was relatively little variation in beef carcass prices, the average monthly price of beef loins—which produce sirloin, Porterhouse, T-bone, and club steaks—varied within a range of about 14½ cents per pound. This is because steaks are most popular in the summer cook-out season, while roasts are in greatest demand in cold weather.

ITEM	AVERAGE 1968 PRICE PER POUND (New York Carlot)
Carcass	$ .46
Hindquarter	.54
Forequarter	.37
Round	.54
Loin	.76
Rib	.61
Arm chuck	.37

Wholesomeness

Meat that has passed Federal inspection for wholesomeness is stamped with a round purple mark, "U.S. INSP'D & P'S'D". The mark is put on carcasses and major cuts, so may not appear on such cuts as roasts and steaks.

INSPECTION MARK

All meat processed in plants which sell their products across State lines must, under Federal law, be inspected for wholesomeness by USDA inspectors. USDA inspectors also supervise the cleanliness and operating procedures of these meat packing plants to make sure that meat is not contaminated or adulterated.

Many States operate their own inspection programs for plants that produce meat for sale within State lines. The State programs must be certified by USDA as equal to the Federal program. In States without inspection programs, USDA inspects all meat plants. This Federal and State activity is aimed at a nationally uniform wholesome meat supply for consumers.

Quality

Quite apart from the wholesomeness of meat is its quality. Meat can be wholesome but at the same time of low quality. Do not be misled by implications that USDA inspection is assurance of **quality**—that is the function of another USDA service, meat grading.

GRADE MARK

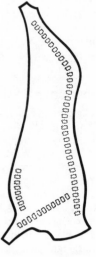

The shield-shaped USDA grade mark is a guide to the **quality** of meat—its tenderness, juiciness, and flavor — while the round inspection mark is assurance of **wholesomeness.**

The U.S. Department of Agriculture provides both inspection and grading services. Inspection, as explained above, is required under Federal law for meat to be sold in interstate commerce. Grading is a voluntary service offered to packers, and others, who pay a fee for the service.

USDA has quality grades for beef, calf, veal, lamb, yearling mutton, and mutton. It also has grades for pork, but these do not carry through to the retail level as do the grades for other kinds of meat.

USDA meat grades, such as U.S. Prime, U.S. Choice, U.S. Good, are based on nationally uniform, Federal standards of quality. They are applied by experienced USDA graders, who are checked constantly by supervisors who travel throughout the country to make sure that all graders are interpreting and applying the standards in a uniform manner. Therefore, you can be sure that a U.S. Choice rib roast, for example, will provide the same good eating no matter where or when you buy it.

Only meat which has first passed inspection for wholesomeness may be graded—so when you see the purple, shield-shaped USDA grade mark it tells you two things: the quality of the meat, and the fact that it has passed inspection for wholesomeness.

The grade mark is applied with a roller stamp, and it is rolled on in a long ribbon-like imprint the length of the carcass and across the shoulders, so that it will appear on most retail cuts if not trimmed off. Ask to see the grade mark when you're buying meat for your freezer —before the meat is cut and trimmed, which may result in the removal of most of the grade marks.

Know Your Dealer

Comparing costs—and making sure you are getting a good value—can be difficult when you are buying a product with which you are unfamiliar. And most consumers are unfamiliar with meats in carcass form.

Your first consideration should be to find a dealer who has a well-established reputation for honesty and fairness. Check with your local Better Business Bureau or Chamber of Commerce if you are not sure.

Although most businessmen are honest, there are always some who will take advantage of the uninformed—and there are a few practices that you should be particularly on guard against.

The old game of "bait and switch" has sprung up in recent years among some dealers who offer meat for the home freezer. This takes the form of offering meat at very low prices, sometimes advertising it as "USDA Choice" or "USDA Prime." Having attracted the customer to his establishment, the dealer will show him the "advertised" carcass. This often will be an overfat, wasty carcass. It may, in fact, be graded "USDA Choice," but be a specially selected wasty specimen which is not typical of the grade. (See section on yield grades.)

Hanging alongside this wasty specimen, however, will be another, leaner carcass which the dealer then will convince the customer is what he really wants for his family. And of course, the price per pound will be much higher. Even though this carcass may not carry the advertised "USDA Prime" or "USDA Choice" grade mark, the dealer may assure the customer that it has been graded or that it is "Fancy," "Supreme," or some other likely sounding "grade" name.

Remember that the only official USDA grades for meat are those listed and described in this pamphlet—any others can mean anything—or nothing. (USDA grades for other products—such as U.S. Grade A for poultry and dairy products and U.S. Fancy for canned fruits and vegetables **cannot** be applied to meat.)

Another practice to watch out for is substituting cuts from the forequarter for hindquarter cuts —and substituting lower grades of meat for higher grades. One customer complained to the USDA about the amount of chuck roast he got when he purchased a hindquarter. (Consult the carcass chart and you will see that the chuck is part of the forequarter.)

Some suppliers advertise a "beef bundle" or a "steak package." Unless these ads specify the grade of the meat and the kind and amount of the various cuts included, you would be well advised to buy with caution.

In general, beware of advertisements which offer "something for nothing"—bargains which are too sensational to believe. No dealer can afford to give meat away, and reputable ones will not pretend to do so.

BEEF CHART

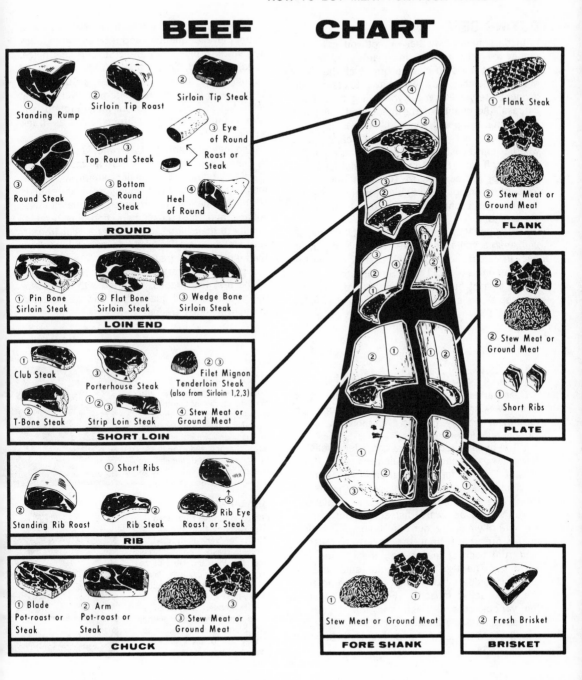

ROUND
① Standing Rump
② Sirloin Tip Roast
② Sirloin Tip Steak
③ Eye of Round Roast or Steak
③ Top Round Steak
③ Round Steak
③ Bottom Round Steak
④ Heel of Round

LOIN END
① Pin Bone Sirloin Steak
② Flat Bone Sirloin Steak
③ Wedge Bone Sirloin Steak

SHORT LOIN
① Club Steak
③ Porterhouse Steak
②③ Filet Mignon Tenderloin Steak (also from Sirloin 1,2,3)
①②③ T-Bone Steak
①②③ Strip Loin Steak
④ Stew Meat or Ground Meat

RIB
① Short Ribs
② Standing Rib Roast
② Rib Steak
② Rib Eye Roast or Steak

CHUCK
① Blade Pot-roast or Steak
② Arm Pot-roast or Steak
③ Stew Meat or Ground Meat

FLANK
① Flank Steak
② Stew Meat or Ground Meat

PLATE
② Stew Meat or Ground Meat
① Short Ribs

FORE SHANK
① Stew Meat or Ground Meat

BRISKET
② Fresh Brisket

BUYING BEEF

In determining whether or not you can save money by buying meat in quantity, over and above what it would cost to buy it at the retail store, remember you will have to take into account the yield of meat you will get from the carcass, the quality of the meat, and the costs of cutting, wrapping, and quick-freezing. You should find out, when buying carcass meat, whether these costs are included in the price per pound, or if you'll have to pay additional for them. The usual charge is 8 to 10 cents per pound for cutting, wrapping, and quick-freezing, whether it is charged separately or added onto the price per pound.

On page 102, you will find a chart which will enable you to compare the cost of buying beef in carcass form with the cost of buying the same amounts of retail cuts. Similar comparisons of the cost of buying retail cuts vs. quarters or wholesale cuts can be made by using the tables on page 96.

Each USDA beef grade is a measure of a distinct level of quality—and it takes eight grades to span the range. They are: USDA Prime, Choice, Good, Standard, Commercial, Utility, Cutter, and Canner. The three lower grades, USDA Utility, Cutter, and Canner, are seldom if ever sold at retail but are used instead to make ground beef and manufactured meat items such as frankfurters.

The highest grade, USDA Prime, is used mostly by hotels and restaurants, but a small amount is sold at retail and by dealers supplying freezer meat. The grade most widely sold at retail is USDA Choice. It is produced in the greatest volume and most consumers find this level of quality to their liking. In buying for your freezer, you would be well advised to select beef from the higher quality grades.

Pictured below are porterhouse steaks in each of the first five grades, together with a description of the level of quality that can be expected in each of those grades.

QUALITY GRADES

Beef varies in quality more than any other meat. Making sure of the quality you get when you buy in quantity, then, is even more important for beef than for other meats.

USDA quality grades offer a consistent, reliable guide to the tenderness, juiciness, and flavor of beef. That is, for any given cut—for example, a sirloin steak—the higher the grade, the greater the degree of tenderness, juiciness, and flavor.

You should be aware that some cuts of beef are naturally more tender than others. The most tender are those from the less used muscles along the back of the animal, the rib and loin sections. The less tender cuts, such as the chuck (shoulder), flank, and round, come from the more active muscles. For a discussion of the various cuts of beef, and the degree of tenderness associated with each, in each grade, see "How to Buy Beef Roasts and Beef Steaks," pages 73-84.

USDA PRIME
Prime grade beef is the ultimate in tenderness, juiciness, and flavor. It has abundant marbling—flecks of fat within the lean—which enhances both flavor and juiciness. Prime roasts and steaks are unexcelled for dry-heat cooking—roasting and broiling.

USDA CHOICE
Choice grade beef has slightly less marbling than Prime, but still is of very high quality. Choice roasts and steaks from the loin and rib will be very tender, juicy, and flavorful and are, like Prime, suited to dry-heat cooking. Many of the less tender cuts, such as those from the rump, round, and blade chuck, can also, if they are USDA Choice, be cooked with dry heat.

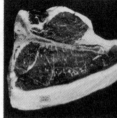

USDA GOOD

Good grade beef often pleases thrifty shoppers because it is somewhat more lean than the higher grades. It is fairly tender, but because it has less marbling it lacks some of the juiciness and flavor of the higher grades. Some retailers sell this quality of beef under a "house" brand or private label rather than the USDA grade name.

YIELD GRADES

As mentioned earlier in this booklet, the yield of usable meat from a beef carcass can vary greatly—regardless of quality grade. This variation is caused, primarily, by differences in the amount of fat on the outside of the carcass. USDA has grades to measure this yield—they are called yield grades and they are designated numerically. Yield Grade 1 denotes the highest yield, and Yield Grade 5 the lowest.

USDA STANDARD

Standard grade beef has a high proportion of lean meat and very little fat. Because it comes from young animals, beef of this grade is fairly tender. But because it lacks marbling, it has less flavor than the higher grades and most cuts will be somewhat dry unless prepared with moist heat.

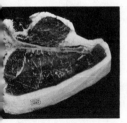

USDA COMMERCIAL

Commercial grade beef is produced only from mature animals—the higher grades are restricted to young animals. Because Commercial grade beef comes from older animals, it is not naturally tender—even though it is well-marbled and could be mistaken by the uninformed for Prime grade (compare the pictures). Commercial grade beef requires long, slow cooking with moist heat to make it tender. But when prepared in this manner it can provide delicious and economical meat dishes—and it will have the rich, full flavor characteristic of mature beef.

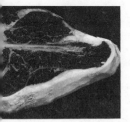

HOW TO FIGURE RETAIL VALUE OF BEEF PURCHASED IN CARCASS FORM (AND MAKE COMPARISONS)

Note: To make realistic comparisons it is necessary to know both the quality grade and the yield grade of the carcass. The higher the quality the more a carcass is worth; likewise, the higher the yield grade, the more it is worth, since it will have a higher yield of lean meat. For illustration, this chart shows the yield from a 300-pound USDA Choice, Yield Grade 3, beef side—a type of carcass that is widely sold.

EXAMPLE: Say that you buy a 300 lb. beef side (USDA Choice, Yield Grade 3) for 65¢ a pound, hanging weight (and the price includes cutting, wrapping, and quick freezing).

Cost of carcass purchase: Hanging weight X quoted price=dollars required to buy side. (300 lbs. X 65¢=$195). **But** total usable beef (see below) is only 72.8% of the hanging weight. So, 72.8 X 300 lbs.=218.40 lbs. (usable beef). Therefore, your actual cost per pound for usable beef is $195 ÷ 218.40 lbs.=89.3¢ per pound.

Cost of retail purchases: To figure a comparable average price for retail cuts of equivalent type and quantity, obtain local prices per pound for the retail cuts listed below. Be sure they are the same quality grade—USDA Choice in this example—and comparable in trim. The figures shown reflect cuts with a maximum of ½ inch outside fat and ground beef with about 25% fat. Then multiply each price by the number of pounds shown (second column in the table). Next total the Retail Value column. This would be your total cost, at retail, for the equivalent of a 300 lb. side of beef. To get the average cost per pound, divide this total by 218.4 pounds (the number of pounds of usable beef you would get from a 300 lb. side). Then you will have a retail price-per-pound to compare with the price per pound you would pay for usable meat in a carcass purchase (89.3¢ in this example).

Yield of Retail Cuts	Percent of Carcass (Yield Grade 3)	Pounds	Local Prices per lb.		Retail Value
Round Steak	9.0	27.0		X	=
Rump Roast (Boneless)	3.3	9.9		X	=
Porterhouse, T-Bone,					
Club Steaks	5.1	15.3		X	=
Sirloin Steak	8.3	24.9		X	=
Rib Roast (7" cut)	6.1	18.3		X	=
Blade Chuck Roast	8.9	26.7		X	=
Arm Chuck Roast (Boneless) . .	5.8	17.4		X	=
Ground Beef	11.1	33.3		X	=
Stew Meat	12.3	36.9		X	=
Brisket (Boneless)	2.1	6.3		X	=
Flank Steak	.5	1.5		X	=
Kidney	.3	.9		X	=
Total Retail Cuts	72.8	218.4			
Waste (fat, bone, and shrinkage)	27.2	81.6		X	=
TOTAL	100.0	300.0		X	TOTAL RETAIL VALUE

Consumers who buy only retail cuts need not be concerned about yield grades since these grades apply only to carcasses and wholesale cuts. In buying retail cuts, however, check to see that excess fat and bone have been removed.

But if you are buying carcasses or wholesale cuts, you should know about yield grades, and seek to buy beef which had been yield graded. The shield-shaped yield grade mark can be found stamped once on each quarter or wholesale cut— it is not rolled on the length of the carcass as is the quality grade shield.

Literally, the yield grades measure the yield of boneless, closely trimmed retail cuts from the high-value parts of the carcass, the round, loin, rib, and chuck. However, they also reflect differences in total yield of retail cuts. The following percentages represent expected yields of retail cuts by yield grade.

Yield Grade 1—means the carcass will yield 79.8 percent or more in retail cuts,
Yield Grade 2—75.2 to 79.7 percent,
Yield Grade 3—70.6 to 75.1 percent,
Yield Grade 4—66 to 70.5 percent, and
Yield Grade 5—65.9 percent or less.

Obviously, you can afford to pay somewhat more for a higher-yielding carcass—or if no price differential is charged, you can get more for your money. At mid-1969 prices, the difference in value between USDA Choice carcasses in adjacent yield grades was about 4 cents per pound. For 300-pound sides, this would mean a value difference of $12.

If you cannot buy carcass beef marked with the yield grade, you can get a good idea of the yield by looking at the thickness of the fat covering over the rib eye muscle. Compare the pictures shown of the rib roasts, taken from typical Yield Grade 2 and Yield Grade 4 carcasses.

For a more detailed discussion of yield grades for beef, see "USDA Yield Grades For Beef" (MB—45). It is available free on postcard request from the Office of Information, U.S. Department of Agriculture, Washington, D.C. 20250. Include your Zipcode when writing.

BUYING LAMB

Buying lamb for your freezer presents fewer problems than buying beef—primarily because the quality of lamb is less variable.

But the quality of lamb **does** vary, so it is advisable to buy lamb that has been graded by the U.S. Department of Agriculture. Since it is produced from young animals, most cuts of USDA Prime or Choice lamb are tender and can be oven roasted or broiled. Lower grades of lamb (USDA Good, Utility and Cull) are seldom marked with the grade when sold at retail.

Pictured are lamb rib chops in the two top grades, together with a description of the quality level that can be expected in each of these grades.

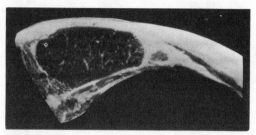

USDA PRIME
Prime grade lamb is very high in tenderness, juiciness, and flavor. It has moderate marbling—flecks of fat within the lean—which enhances both flavor and juiciness. Prime chops and roasts are excellent for dry-heat cooking —broiling and roasting.

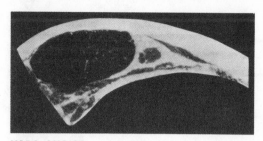

USDA CHOICE
Choice grade lamb has slightly less marbling than Prime, but still is of very high quality. Like Prime, Choice chops and roasts are very tender, juicy and flavorful and suited to dry-heat cooking.

LAMB CHART

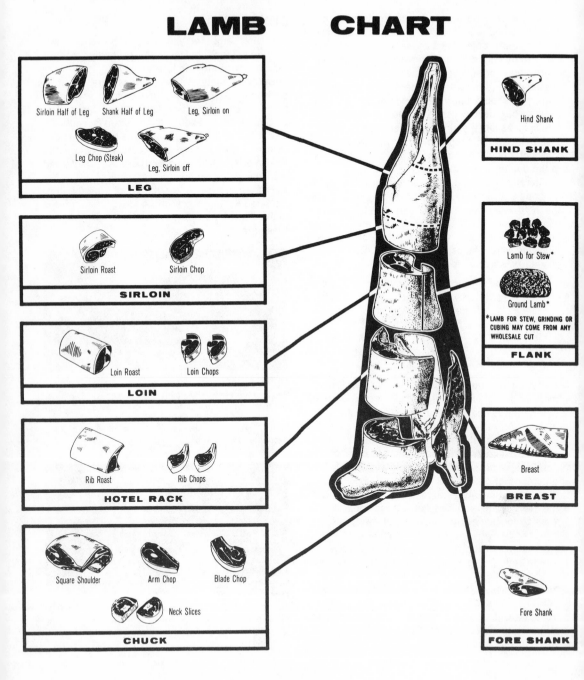

LEG
Sirloin Half of Leg   Shank Half of Leg   Leg, Sirloin on
Leg Chop (Steak)   Leg, Sirloin off

SIRLOIN
Sirloin Roast   Sirloin Chop

LOIN
Loin Roast   Loin Chops

HOTEL RACK
Rib Roast   Rib Chops

CHUCK
Square Shoulder   Arm Chop   Blade Chop
Neck Slices

HIND SHANK
Hind Shank

FLANK
Lamb for Stew*
Ground Lamb*
*LAMB FOR STEW, GRINDING OR CUBING MAY COME FROM ANY WHOLESALE CUT

BREAST
Breast

FORE SHANK
Fore Shank

Lamb is produced from animals less than a year old. Meat from older sheep is called yearling mutton or mutton, and if it is graded these words will be stamped on the meat along with the shield-shaped grade mark. In that way, you can be sure whether you're getting lamb, yearling mutton, or mutton.

Grades for yearling mutton and mutton are the same as for lamb, except that mutton does not qualify for the Prime grade.

Yield Grades

The U.S. Department of Agriculture also has yield grades for lamb. Like beef yield grades, yield grades for lamb measure the ratio of lean meat to fat and bone. The same rating system of five yield grades is used—with Yield Grade 1 representing the highest yield of lean meat, and Yield Grade 5 the lowest.

Generally, variations in the yield result primarily from differences in fatness on the outside of the carcass and in fat deposited on the inside of the carcass. You should be aware that there are considerable differences in the meat yield between carcasses in the same quality grade, and steer clear of those with a large amount of excess fat. The pictures below, of two lamb rib chops, illustrate an extreme variation in the amount of fat covering. Studies by USDA in 1968 indicated a value difference between carcasses of adjacent yield grades of about 3½ cents per pound.

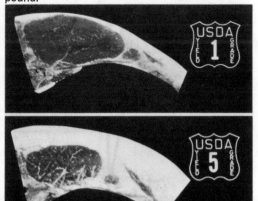

YIELD OF CUTS FROM YIELD GRADE 3 LAMB CARCASSES*

Retail Cuts	Percent of Carcass	Pounds
Loin Chops	16.5	8.25
Rib Chops	8.2	4.10
Legs		
(Short Cut)	20.5	10.25
Shoulder Roast ...	22.3	11.15
Foreshanks	3.1	1.55
Breast	7.9	3.95
Flank	2.9	1.45
Stew Meat	1.9	.95
Kidney	.5	.25
Total Usable Retail Cuts	83.8	41.90
Waste (fat, bone, shrinkage)	16.2	8.10
TOTAL	100.0	50.00

Note: To compare the price of a lamb carcass with the cost of buying the same amount of retail cuts, you can use the table above to construct a chart like the one for beef on page 96.

* Based on cutting test conducted by USDA in cooperation with a major retailer.

BUYING PORK

Like lamb, pork is generally produced from young animals and is therefore less variable in quality than beef.

U.S. Department of Agriculture grades for pork reflect only two levels of quality—acceptable and unacceptable. Unacceptable quality pork—which includes that having meat that is soft and watery—is graded U.S. Utility. All higher grades must have acceptable quality of lean meat. The differences between these higher grades which are numerical, ranging from U.S. No. 1 to U.S. No. 4, are solely those of yield of the four major lean cuts. In this respect they are similar to the yield grades for beef and for lamb.

Like the yield grades for beef and for lamb, the grades for pork are not of concern to the consumer who buys pork at the retail store and the grades are not identified at the retail level. But they can be useful if you buy pork in carcass form.

PORK CHART

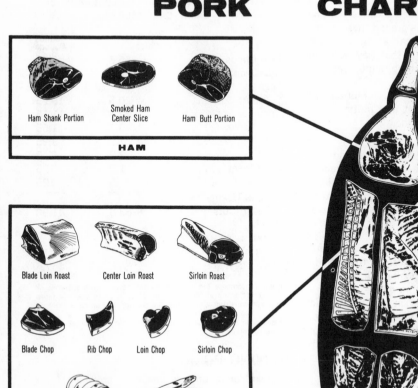

HAM

Ham Shank Portion

Smoked Ham
Center Slice

Ham Butt Portion

LOIN

Blade Loin Roast

Center Loin Roast

Sirloin Roast

Blade Chop

Rib Chop

Loin Chop

Sirloin Chop

Rolled
Loin Roast

Tenderloin

BOSTON BUTT

Boston Butt

Blade Steak

Rolled
Boston Butt

BELLY

Spareribs

Slab Bacon

Sliced Bacon

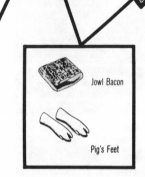

Jowl Bacon

Pig's Feet

PICNIC

Picnic

Arm Roast

Arm Steak

Hock

Little grading of pork carcasses is presently being done, but it may be possible to order by grade through a wholesale meat dealer. A U.S. No. 1 pork carcass will yield more than 53 percent of its weight in the four major lean cuts, the ham, loin, Boston butt, and picnic shoulder. A U.S. No. 2 will yield 50–53 percent in those cuts; U.S. No. 3, 47–50 percent, and U.S. No. 4, less than 47 percent.

If you're thinking of buying a pork carcass or side, you'll want to get it from a place that is equipped to render the lard and cure the bacon, hams, and other cuts that you may not want to use fresh. If you cannot obtain this service, you would probably find it better to buy wholesale cuts of fresh pork, such as shoulders, loins, and hams.

In buying pork, look for cuts with a relatively small amount of fat over the outside and with meat that is firm and a grayish pink color. For best eating, the meat should have a small amount of marbling.

HOW MUCH SHOULD I BUY?

How much meat you should buy at any one time depends, of course, on how much you want to spend at one time, the amount of freezer storage space you have available, and how much your family consumes. You will need to do some figuring.

Properly wrapped meat cuts, stored at 0 degrees F., or lower, will maintain their quality for a long time. This varies, however, with the kind of meat. In the table below, the times indicated represent a range within which you can store the meat with reasonable expectation that it will maintain its quality. Meats can be kept safely frozen for longer periods than indicated, but they are apt to lose quality.

SUGGESTED STORAGE TIMES
FOR MEAT AT 0° F.

Beef	8–12 months
Lamb	8–12 months
Pork, fresh	4–8 months
Ground beef and lamb	3–4 months
Pork Sausage	1–3 months

On the average, one cubic foot of freezer space will accommodate 35 to 40 pounds of cut and wrapped meat, though it will be slightly less if the meat is packaged in odd shapes.

Meat should be initially frozen at —10°F. or lower, and as quickly as possible. If you are freezing it yourself, allow some space for air to circulate between the packages.

The amount of food frozen at one time should be limited in order to get as quick and efficient freezing as possible. Only the amount of unfrozen food that will freeze within 24 hours should be put into the freezer. Usually that will be about 2 or 3 pounds to each cubic foot of freezer capacity. The speed of freezing will be slower if the freezer is overloaded with unfrozen food.

For large meat purchases, it is usually best to get the freezing done by a commercial establishment properly equipped to do the job. Quick freezing causes less damage to the meat fibers. Slower freezing causes more of the cells to rupture, due to formation of large ice crystals, so that more meat juices are lost when the meat is thawed.

Proper wrapping of meat for the freezer is as important as proper storage. Use a moisture-vapor-proof wrap, such as heavy aluminum foil, heavily waxed freezer paper, or specially laminated papers. Wrap the meat closely, eliminating all air if possible. Double thicknesses of waxed paper should be placed between chops and steaks to prevent their sticking together. Seal the packages well and mark them with the date. The rule in using frozen meat should be: First in, first out.

Improperly wrapped packages will allow air to enter and draw moisture from the meat, resulting in "freezer burn" or meat which is dry and less flavorful.

It is perfectly safe to refreeze meat that has been kept refrigerated after thawing. However, refreezing of defrosted meat is not usually recommended because there is some loss of meat quality.

A CATALOGUE OF SELECTED DOVER BOOKS
IN ALL FIELDS OF INTEREST

A CATALOGUE OF SELECTED DOVER BOOKS
IN ALL FIELDS OF INTEREST

AMERICA'S OLD MASTERS, James T. Flexner. Four men emerged unexpectedly from provincial 18th century America to leadership in European art: Benjamin West, J. S. Copley, C. R. Peale, Gilbert Stuart. Brilliant coverage of lives and contributions. Revised, 1967 edition. 69 plates. 365pp. of text.
21806-6 Paperbound $3.00

FIRST FLOWERS OF OUR WILDERNESS: AMERICAN PAINTING, THE COLONIAL PERIOD, James T. Flexner. Painters, and regional painting traditions from earliest Colonial times up to the emergence of Copley, West and Peale Sr., Foster, Gustavus Hesselius, Feke, John Smibert and many anonymous painters in the primitive manner. Engaging presentation, with 162 illustrations. xxii + 368pp.
22180-6 Paperbound $3.50

THE LIGHT OF DISTANT SKIES: AMERICAN PAINTING, 1760-1835, James T. Flexner. The great generation of early American painters goes to Europe to learn and to teach: West, Copley, Gilbert Stuart and others. Allston, Trumbull, Morse; also contemporary American painters—primitives, derivatives, academics—who remained in America. 102 illustrations. xiii + 306pp.
22179-2 Paperbound $3.50

A HISTORY OF THE RISE AND PROGRESS OF THE ARTS OF DESIGN IN THE UNITED STATES, William Dunlap. Much the richest mine of information on early American painters, sculptors, architects, engravers, miniaturists, etc. The only source of information for scores of artists, the major primary source for many others. Unabridged reprint of rare original 1834 edition, with new introduction by James T. Flexner, and 394 new illustrations. Edited by Rita Weiss. 6⅝ x 9⅝.
21695-0, 21696-9, 21697-7 Three volumes, Paperbound $15.00

EPOCHS OF CHINESE AND JAPANESE ART, Ernest F. Fenollosa. From primitive Chinese art to the 20th century, thorough history, explanation of every important art period and form, including Japanese woodcuts; main stress on China and Japan, but Tibet, Korea also included. Still unexcelled for its detailed, rich coverage of cultural background, aesthetic elements, diffusion studies, particularly of the historical period. 2nd, 1913 edition. 242 illustrations. lii + 439pp. of text.
20364-6, 20365-4 Two volumes, Paperbound $6.00

THE GENTLE ART OF MAKING ENEMIES, James A. M. Whistler. Greatest wit of his day deflates Oscar Wilde, Ruskin, Swinburne; strikes back at inane critics, exhibitions, art journalism; aesthetics of impressionist revolution in most striking form. Highly readable classic by great painter. Reproduction of edition designed by Whistler. Introduction by Alfred Werner. xxxvi + 334pp.
21875-9 Paperbound $3.00

THE PRINCIPLES OF PSYCHOLOGY, William James. The famous long course, complete and unabridged. Stream of thought, time perception, memory, experimental methods—these are only some of the concerns of a work that was years ahead of its time and still valid, interesting, useful. 94 figures. Total of xviii + 1391pp.
20381-6, 20382-4 Two volumes, Paperbound $9.00

THE STRANGE STORY OF THE QUANTUM, Banesh Hoffmann. Non-mathematical but thorough explanation of work of Planck, Einstein, Bohr, Pauli, de Broglie, Schrödinger, Heisenberg, Dirac, Feynman, etc. No technical background needed. "Of books attempting such an account, this is the best," Henry Margenau, Yale. 40-page "Postscript 1959." xii + 285pp.
20518-5 Paperbound $3.00

THE RISE OF THE NEW PHYSICS, A. d'Abro. Most thorough explanation in print of central core of mathematical physics, both classical and modern; from Newton to Dirac and Heisenberg. Both history and exposition; philosophy of science, causality, explanations of higher mathematics, analytical mechanics, electromagnetism, thermodynamics, phase rule, special and general relativity, matrices. No higher mathematics needed to follow exposition, though treatment is elementary to intermediate in level. Recommended to serious student who wishes verbal understanding. 97 illustrations. xvii + 982pp.
20003-5, 20004-3 Two volumes, Paperbound $10.00

GREAT IDEAS OF OPERATIONS RESEARCH, Jagjit Singh. Easily followed non-technical explanation of mathematical tools, aims, results: statistics, linear programming, game theory, queueing theory, Monte Carlo simulation, etc. Uses only elementary mathematics. Many case studies, several analyzed in detail. Clarity, breadth make this excellent for specialist in another field who wishes background. 41 figures. x + 228pp.
21886-4 Paperbound $2.50

GREAT IDEAS OF MODERN MATHEMATICS: THEIR NATURE AND USE, Jagjit Singh. Internationally famous expositor, winner of Unesco's Kalinga Award for science popularization explains verbally such topics as differential equations, matrices, groups, sets, transformations, mathematical logic and other important modern mathematics, as well as use in physics, astrophysics, and similar fields. Superb exposition for layman, scientist in other areas. viii + 312pp.
20587-8 Paperbound $2.75

GREAT IDEAS IN INFORMATION THEORY, LANGUAGE AND CYBERNETICS, Jagjit Singh. The analog and digital computers, how they work, how they are like and unlike the human brain, the men who developed them, their future applications, computer terminology. An essential book for today, even for readers with little math. Some mathematical demonstrations included for more advanced readers. 118 figures. Tables. ix + 338pp.
21694-2 Paperbound $2.50

CHANCE, LUCK AND STATISTICS, Horace C. Levinson. Non-mathematical presentation of fundamentals of probability theory and science of statistics and their applications. Games of chance, betting odds, misuse of statistics, normal and skew distributions, birth rates, stock speculation, insurance. Enlarged edition. Formerly "The Science of Chance." xiii + 357pp.
21007-3 Paperbound $2.50

ADVENTURES OF AN AFRICAN SLAVER, Theodore Canot. Edited by Brantz Mayer. A detailed portrayal of slavery and the slave trade, 1820-1840. Canot, an established trader along the African coast, describes the slave economy of the African kingdoms, the treatment of captured negroes, the extensive journeys in the interior to gather slaves, slave revolts and their suppression, harems, bribes, and much more. Full and unabridged republication of 1854 edition. Introduction by Malcom Cowley. 16 illustrations. xvii + 448pp.   22456-2 Paperbound $3.50

MY BONDAGE AND MY FREEDOM, Frederick Douglass. Born and brought up in slavery, Douglass witnessed its horrors and experienced its cruelties, but went on to become one of the most outspoken forces in the American anti-slavery movement. Considered the best of his autobiographies, this book graphically describes the inhuman treatment of slaves, its effects on slave owners and slave families, and how Douglass's determination led him to a new life. Unaltered reprint of 1st (1855) edition. xxxii + 464pp.   22457-0 Paperbound $3.50

THE INDIANS' BOOK, recorded and edited by Natalie Curtis. Lore, music, narratives, dozens of drawings by Indians themselves from an authoritative and important survey of native culture among Plains, Southwestern, Lake and Pueblo Indians. Standard work in popular ethnomusicology. 149 songs in full notation. 23 drawings, 23 photos. xxxi + 584pp. 6⅝ x 9⅜.   21939-9 Paperbound $5.00

DICTIONARY OF AMERICAN PORTRAITS, edited by Hayward and Blanche Cirker. 4024 portraits of 4000 most important Americans, colonial days to 1905 (with a few important categories, like Presidents, to present). Pioneers, explorers, colonial figures, U. S. officials, politicians, writers, military and naval men, scientists, inventors, manufacturers, jurists, actors, historians, educators, notorious figures, Indian chiefs, etc. All authentic contemporary likenesses. The only work of its kind in existence; supplements all biographical sources for libraries. Indispensable to anyone working with American history. 8,000-item classified index, finding lists, other aids. xiv + 756pp. 9¼ x 12¾.   21823-6 Clothbound $30.00

TRITTON'S GUIDE TO BETTER WINE AND BEER MAKING FOR BEGINNERS, S. M. Tritton. All you need to know to make family-sized quantities of over 100 types of grape, fruit, herb and vegetable wines; as well as beers, mead, cider, etc. Complete recipes, advice as to equipment, procedures such as fermenting, bottling, and storing wines. Recipes given in British, U. S., and metric measures. Accompanying booklet lists sources in U. S. A. where ingredients may be bought, and additional information. 11 illustrations. 157pp. 5⅝ x 8⅛.
22090-7   **Paperbound $2.00**

GARDENING WITH HERBS FOR FLAVOR AND FRAGRANCE, Helen M. Fox. How to grow herbs in your own garden, how to use them in your cooking (over 55 recipes included), legends and myths associated with each species, uses in medicine, perfumes, etc.—these are elements of one of the few books written especially for American herb fanciers. Guides you step-by-step from soil preparation to harvesting and storage for each type of herb. 12 drawings by Louise Mansfield. xiv + 334pp.
22540-2 Paperbound $2.50

AMERICAN FOOD AND GAME FISHES, David S. Jordan and Barton W. Evermann. Definitive source of information, detailed and accurate enough to enable the sportsman and nature lover to identify conclusively some 1,000 species and sub-species of North American fish, sought for food or sport. Coverage of range, physiology, habits, life history, food value. Best methods of capture, interest to the angler, advice on bait, fly-fishing, etc. 338 drawings and photographs. l + 574pp. 6⅝ x 9⅜.
22196-2 Paperbound $5.00

THE FROG BOOK, Mary C. Dickerson. Complete with extensive finding keys, over 300 photographs, and an introduction to the general biology of frogs and toads, this is the classic non-technical study of Northeastern and Central species. 58 species; 290 photographs and 16 color plates. xvii + 253pp.
21973-9 Paperbound $4.00

THE MOTH BOOK: A GUIDE TO THE MOTHS OF NORTH AMERICA, William J. Holland. Classical study, eagerly sought after and used for the past 60 years. Clear identification manual to more than 2,000 different moths, largest manual in existence. General information about moths, capturing, mounting, classifying, etc., followed by species by species descriptions. 263 illustrations plus 48 color plates show almost every species, full size. 1968 edition, preface, nomenclature changes by A. E. Brower. xxiv + 479pp. of text. 6½ x 9¼.
21948-8 Paperbound $6.00

THE SEA-BEACH AT EBB-TIDE, Augusta Foote Arnold. Interested amateur can identify hundreds of marine plants and animals on coasts of North America; marine algae; seaweeds; squids; hermit crabs; horse shoe crabs; shrimps; corals; sea anemones; etc. Species descriptions cover: structure; food; reproductive cycle; size; shape; color; habitat; etc. Over 600 drawings. 85 plates. xii + 490pp.
21949-6 Paperbound $4.00

COMMON BIRD SONGS, Donald J. Borror. 33⅓ 12-inch record presents songs of 60 important birds of the eastern United States. A thorough, serious record which provides several examples for each bird, showing different types of song, individual variations, etc. Inestimable identification aid for birdwatcher. 32-page booklet gives text about birds and songs, with illustration for each bird.
21829-5 Record, book, album. Monaural. $3.50

FADS AND FALLACIES IN THE NAME OF SCIENCE, Martin Gardner. Fair, witty appraisal of cranks and quacks of science: Atlantis, Lemuria, hollow earth, flat earth, Velikovsky, orgone energy, Dianetics, flying saucers, Bridey Murphy, food fads, medical fads, perpetual motion, etc. Formerly "In the Name of Science." x + 363pp.
20394-8 Paperbound $3.00

HOAXES, Curtis D. MacDougall. Exhaustive, unbelievably rich account of great hoaxes: Locke's moon hoax, Shakespearean forgeries, sea serpents, Loch Ness monster, Cardiff giant, John Wilkes Booth's mummy, Disumbrationist school of art, dozens more; also journalism, psychology of hoaxing. 54 illustrations. xi + 338pp.
20465-0 Paperbound $3.50

DESIGN BY ACCIDENT; A BOOK OF "ACCIDENTAL EFFECTS" FOR ARTISTS AND DESIGNERS, James F. O'Brien. Create your own unique, striking, imaginative effects by "controlled accident" interaction of materials: paints and lacquers, oil and water based paints, splatter, crackling materials, shatter, similar items. Everything you do will be different; first book on this limitless art, so useful to both fine artist and commercial artist. Full instructions. 192 plates showing "accidents," 8 in color. viii + 215pp. 8⅜ x 11¼. 21942-9 Paperbound $3.75

THE BOOK OF SIGNS, Rudolf Koch. Famed German type designer draws 493 beautiful symbols: religious, mystical, alchemical, imperial, property marks, runes, etc. Remarkable fusion of traditional and modern. Good for suggestions of timelessness, smartness, modernity. Text. vi + 104pp. 6⅛ x 9¼. 20162-7 Paperbound $1.50

HISTORY OF INDIAN AND INDONESIAN ART, Ananda K. Coomaraswamy. An unabridged republication of one of the finest books by a great scholar in Eastern art. Rich in descriptive material, history, social backgrounds; Sunga reliefs, Rajput paintings, Gupta temples, Burmese frescoes, textiles, jewelry, sculpture, etc. 400 photos. viii + 423pp. 6⅜ x 9¾. 21436-2 Paperbound $5.00

PRIMITIVE ART, Franz Boas. America's foremost anthropologist surveys textiles, ceramics, woodcarving, basketry, metalwork, etc.; patterns, technology, creation of symbols, style origins. All areas of world, but very full on Northwest Coast Indians. More than 350 illustrations of baskets, boxes, totem poles, weapons, etc. 378 pp. 20025-6 Paperbound $3.00

THE GENTLEMAN AND CABINET MAKER'S DIRECTOR, Thomas Chippendale. Full reprint (third edition, 1762) of most influential furniture book of all time, by master cabinetmaker. 200 plates, illustrating chairs, sofas, mirrors, tables, cabinets, plus 24 photographs of surviving pieces. Biographical introduction by N. Bienenstock. vi + 249pp. 9⅞ x 12¾. 21601-2 Paperbound $5.00

AMERICAN ANTIQUE FURNITURE, Edgar G. Miller, Jr. The basic coverage of all American furniture before 1840. Individual chapters cover type of furniture—clocks, tables, sideboards, etc.—chronologically, with inexhaustible wealth of data. More than 2100 photographs, all identified, commented on. Essential to all early American collectors. Introduction by H. E. Keyes. vi + 1106pp. 7⅞ x 10¾. 21599-7, 21600-4 Two volumes, Paperbound $11.00

PENNSYLVANIA DUTCH AMERICAN FOLK ART, Henry J. Kauffman. 279 photos, 28 drawings of tulipware, Fraktur script, painted tinware, toys, flowered furniture, quilts, samplers, hex signs, house interiors, etc. Full descriptive text. Excellent for tourist, rewarding for designer, collector. Map. 146pp. 7⅞ x 10¾. 21205-X Paperbound $3.00

EARLY NEW ENGLAND GRAVESTONE RUBBINGS, Edmund V. Gillon, Jr. 43 photographs, 226 carefully reproduced rubbings show heavily symbolic, sometimes macabre early gravestones, up to early 19th century. Remarkable early American primitive art, occasionally strikingly beautiful; always powerful. Text. xxvi + 207pp. 8⅜ x 11¼. 21380-3 Paperbound $4.00

THE ARCHITECTURE OF COUNTRY HOUSES, Andrew J. Downing. Together with Vaux's *Villas and Cottages* this is the basic book for Hudson River Gothic architecture of the middle Victorian period. Full, sound discussions of general aspects of housing, architecture, style, decoration, furnishing, together with scores of detailed house plans, illustrations of specific buildings, accompanied by full text. Perhaps the most influential single American architectural book. 1850 edition. Introduction by J. Stewart Johnson. 321 figures, 34 architectural designs. xvi + 560pp.
22003-6 Paperbound $5.00

LOST EXAMPLES OF COLONIAL ARCHITECTURE, John Mead Howells. Full-page photographs of buildings that have disappeared or been so altered as to be denatured, including many designed by major early American architects. 245 plates. xvii + 248pp. 7⅞ x 10¾.
21143-6 Paperbound $3.50

DOMESTIC ARCHITECTURE OF THE AMERICAN COLONIES AND OF THE EARLY REPUBLIC, Fiske Kimball. Foremost architect and restorer of Williamsburg and Monticello covers nearly 200 homes between 1620-1825. Architectural details, construction, style features, special fixtures, floor plans, etc. Generally considered finest work in its area. 219 illustrations of houses, doorways, windows, capital mantels. xx + 314pp. 7⅞ x 10¾.
21743-4 Paperbound $4.00

EARLY AMERICAN ROOMS: 1650-1858, edited by Russell Hawes Kettell. Tour of 12 rooms, each representative of a different era in American history and each furnished, decorated, designed and occupied in the style of the era. 72 plans and elevations, 8-page color section, etc., show fabrics, wall papers, arrangements, etc. Full descriptive text. xvii + 200pp. of text. 8⅜ x 11¼.
21633-0 Paperbound $5.00

THE FITZWILLIAM VIRGINAL BOOK, edited by J. Fuller Maitland and W. B. Squire. Full modern printing of famous early 17th-century ms. volume of 300 works by Morley, Byrd, Bull, Gibbons, etc. For piano or other modern keyboard instrument; easy to read format. xxxvi + 938pp. 8⅜ x 11.
21068-5, 21069-3 Two volumes, Paperbound $12.00

KEYBOARD MUSIC, Johann Sebastian Bach. Bach Gesellschaft edition. A rich selection of Bach's masterpieces for the harpsichord: the six English Suites, six French Suites, the six Partitas (Clavierübung part I), the Goldberg Variations (Clavierübung part IV), the fifteen Two-Part Inventions and the fifteen Three-Part Sinfonias. Clearly reproduced on large sheets with ample margins; eminently playable. vi + 312pp. 8⅛ x 11.
22360-4 Paperbound $5.00

THE MUSIC OF BACH: AN INTRODUCTION, Charles Sanford Terry. A fine, nontechnical introduction to Bach's music, both instrumental and vocal. Covers organ music, chamber music, passion music, other types. Analyzes themes, developments, innovations. x + 114pp.
21075-8 Paperbound $1.95

BEETHOVEN AND HIS NINE SYMPHONIES, Sir George Grove. Noted British musicologist provides best history, analysis, commentary on symphonies. Very thorough, rigorously accurate; necessary to both advanced student and amateur music lover. 436 musical passages. vii + 407 pp.
20334-4 Paperbound $4.00

JOHANN SEBASTIAN BACH, Philipp Spitta. One of the great classics of musicology, this definitive analysis of Bach's music (and life) has never been surpassed. Lucid, nontechnical analyses of hundreds of pieces (30 pages devoted to St. Matthew Passion, 26 to B Minor Mass). Also includes major analysis of 18th-century music. 450 musical examples. 40-page musical supplement. Total of xx + 1799pp.

(EUK) 22278-0, 22279-9 Two volumes, Clothbound $25.00

MOZART AND HIS PIANO CONCERTOS, Cuthbert Girdlestone. The only full-length study of an important area of Mozart's creativity. Provides detailed analyses of all 23 concertos, traces inspirational sources. 417 musical examples. Second edition. 509pp. 21271-8 Paperbound $4.50

THE PERFECT WAGNERITE: A COMMENTARY ON THE NIBLUNG'S RING, George Bernard Shaw. Brilliant and still relevant criticism in remarkable essays on Wagner's Ring cycle, Shaw's ideas on political and social ideology behind the plots, role of Leitmotifs, vocal requisites, etc. Prefaces. xxi + 136pp.

(USO) 21707-8 Paperbound $1.75

DON GIOVANNI, W. A. Mozart. Complete libretto, modern English translation; biographies of composer and librettist; accounts of early performances and critical reaction. Lavishly illustrated. All the material you need to understand and appreciate this great work. Dover Opera Guide and Libretto Series; translated and introduced by Ellen Bleiler. 92 illustrations. 209pp.

21134-7 Paperbound $2.00

BASIC ELECTRICITY, U. S. Bureau of Naval Personel. Originally a training course, best non-technical coverage of basic theory of electricity and its applications. Fundamental concepts, batteries, circuits, conductors and wiring techniques, AC and DC, inductance and capacitance, generators, motors, transformers, magnetic amplifiers, synchros, servomechanisms, etc. Also covers blue-prints, electrical diagrams, etc. Many questions, with answers. 349 illustrations. x + 448pp. 6½ x 9¼.

20973-3 Paperbound $3.50

REPRODUCTION OF SOUND, Edgar Villchur. Thorough coverage for laymen of high fidelity systems, reproducing systems in general, needles, amplifiers, preamps, loudspeakers, feedback, explaining physical background. "A rare talent for making technicalities vividly comprehensible," R. Darrell, *High Fidelity.* 69 figures iv + 92pp. 21515-6 Paperbound $1.35

HEAR ME TALKIN' TO YA: THE STORY OF JAZZ AS TOLD BY THE MEN WHO MADE IT, Nat Shapiro and Nat Hentoff. Louis Armstrong, Fats Waller, Jo Jones, Clarence Williams, Billy Holiday, Duke Ellington, Jelly Roll Morton and dozens of other jazz greats tell how it was in Chicago's South Side, New Orleans, depression Harlem and the modern West Coast as jazz was born and grew. xvi + 429pp.

21726-4 Paperbound $3.95

FABLES OF AESOP, translated by Sir Roger L'Estrange. A reproduction of the very rare 1931 Paris edition; a selection of the most interesting fables, together with 50 imaginative drawings by Alexander Calder. v + 128pp. 6½x9¼.

21780-9 Paperbound $1.50

MATHEMATICAL PUZZLES FOR BEGINNERS AND ENTHUSIASTS, Geoffrey Mott-Smith. 189 puzzles from easy to difficult—involving arithmetic, logic, algebra, properties of digits, probability, etc.—for enjoyment and mental stimulus. Explanation of mathematical principles behind the puzzles. 135 illustrations. viii + 248pp.

20198-8 Paperbound $2.00

PAPER FOLDING FOR BEGINNERS, William D. Murray and Francis J. Rigney. Easiest book on the market, clearest instructions on making interesting, beautiful origami. Sail boats, cups, roosters, frogs that move legs, bonbon boxes, standing birds, etc. 40 projects; more than 275 diagrams and photographs. 94pp.

20713-7 Paperbound $1.00

TRICKS AND GAMES ON THE POOL TABLE, Fred Herrmann. 79 tricks and games— some solitaires, some for two or more players, some competitive games—to entertain you between formal games. Mystifying shots and throws, unusual caroms, tricks involving such props as cork, coins, a hat, etc. Formerly *Fun on the Pool Table*. 77 figures. 95pp.

21814-7 Paperbound $1.25

HAND SHADOWS TO BE THROWN UPON THE WALL: A SERIES OF NOVEL AND AMUSING FIGURES FORMED BY THE HAND, Henry Bursill. Delightful picturebook from great-grandfather's day shows how to make 18 different hand shadows: a bird that flies, duck that quacks, dog that wags his tail, camel, goose, deer, boy, turtle, etc. Only book of its sort. vi + 33pp. $6\frac{1}{2}$ x $9\frac{1}{4}$.   21779-5 Paperbound $1.00

WHITTLING AND WOODCARVING, E. J. Tangerman. 18th printing of best book on market. "If you can cut a potato you can carve" toys and puzzles, chains, chessmen, caricatures, masks, frames, woodcut blocks, surface patterns, much more. Information on tools, woods, techniques. Also goes into serious wood sculpture from Middle Ages to present, East and West. 464 photos, figures. x + 293pp.

20965-2 Paperbound $2.50

HISTORY OF PHILOSOPHY, Julián Marias. Possibly the clearest, most easily followed, best planned, most useful one-volume history of philosophy on the market; neither skimpy nor overfull. Full details on system of every major philosopher and dozens of less important thinkers from pre-Socratics up to Existentialism and later. Strong on many European figures usually omitted. Has gone through dozens of editions in Europe. 1966 edition, translated by Stanley Appelbaum and Clarence Strowbridge. xviii + 505pp.

21739-6 Paperbound $3.50

YOGA: A SCIENTIFIC EVALUATION, Kovoor T. Behanan. Scientific but non-technical study of physiological results of yoga exercises; done under auspices of Yale U. Relations to Indian thought, to psychoanalysis, etc. 16 photos. xxiii + 270pp.

20505-3 Paperbound $2.50

Prices subject to change without notice.
Available at your book dealer or write for free catalogue to Dept. GI, Dover Publications, Inc., 180 Varick St., N. Y., N. Y. 10014. Dover publishes more than 150 books each year on science, elementary and advanced mathematics, biology, music, art, literary history, social sciences and other areas.